LOOKING FOR THE
HORSE LATITUDES

LOOKING FOR THE
HORSE LATITUDES

Miguel Gonzalez-Gerth

HOST PUBLICATIONS
AUSTIN, TEXAS

Host Publications, Inc. 1000 East 7ᵗʰ Street, Suite 201, Austin, TX 78702

Layout and Design: Joe Bratcher & Anand Ramaswamy
Cover Art: Mary Lou Williams
Cover Design: Anand Ramaswamy

First Edition

Library of Congress Cataloging-in-Publication Data

Gonzalez-Gerth, Miguel.
  Looking for the horse latitudes / Miguel Gonzalez-Gerth.
     p. cm.
  ISBN-13: 978-0-924047-49-7 (hardcover : alk. paper)
  ISBN-10: 0-924047-49-6 (hardcover : alk. paper)
  ISBN-13: 978-0-924047-48-0 (pbk. : alk. paper)
  ISBN-10: 0-924047-48-8 (pbk. : alk. paper)
  I. Title.
  PQ7298.17.O459L66 2007
  861'.64--dc22
                                    2007029446

TABLE OF CONTENTS

NAUFRAGIO DE SIRENAS / SHIPWRECK WITH MERMAIDS

THE SPACE OF THE NIGHT

EN BUSCA DE LAS CALMAS ECUATORIALES / LOOKING FOR THE HORSE LATITUDES

ODA A SAFO / ODE TO SAPPHO

GIOVINEZZA / GIOVINEZZA

CLAVES PARA UNA ANUNCIACIÓN /
KEYS TO AN ANNUNCIATION

AUTHOR'S NOTE

When Joe Bratcher invited me to submit a book of my poetry in both Spanish and English, I was, needless to say, extremely flattered. But somehow I did not really expect that the manuscript of this book would turn out to be a sort of laboratory in which a very interesting experiment would be carried out. The experiment has confirmed something about poetry which I had always believed, though somehow unconsciously: that translation, adaptation or imitation (as Robert Lowell used this word) of a poem is and can be no more than approximation of the original. Therefore, the original is the only valid text. Obviously, this is so because poetry resides in a language and every language has its own system of sound, grammatical structures, lexical resources and cultural framework. One cannot expect to be able to render all that equally in another language. The whole intellectual and emotional context varies. In translating poetry the most difficult achievement is to keep the form of the original and still have the result in the second language sound natural. This very seldom can be done in a line by line parallel, so the translator might achieve something else, perhaps even more beautiful, but he will have altered the form and, therefore, the original poem.

So the challenge generally faced by the translator of poetry is fairly well known. But the challenge faced by a poet in trying to replicate his or her own poetry in another language (assuming he or she is equally adept in both languages) is another matter. Any translator must be careful not to translate literally and yet, at the same time, keep the spirit of the original in the new version of what linguists call the target language. By spirit here I refer to the aura of impression, such as it may be, suggested by the original poem when heard or read. The ambilingual poet (as I regard myself) dealing in the transcription of his or her own poetry, though one would assume able to take more liberties, ends up having more trouble in fashioning equivalents. He or she might even be tempted to change radically some or all found in the patch of lyric that was the original. And that is because such poet happens to be uncommonly capable of navigating in the waters of two different languages, both poetical. This is uncommon because he or she must possess what in German is called *Sprachgefühl* (the feeling for a language) in two different realms of expression. And yet such poet will find and have to admit that it was in the language in which the poem was first written where the poetic discoveries were made that amount to revelations, combinations of sounds and images whose equivalents cannot be found in another language, no matter how mastered it may be.

There are several poems in this bilingual collection that evince what I've just written. I have purposely refrained from referring to these texts as translations, although they may be such to some extent. Their peculiar character is that of something like mirror-images somewhat distorted when not the originals. Take, for example, the first pair, "Ashes of the Dead" and its Spanish counterpart. The poem was originally written in English, and the phrase "a columbarium rendered suddenly agape" has no satisfactory equivalent. The next two, "The Mirror´s Face" and "The Other Side of the Map" were first written in Spanish. The careful reader will detect some lapses in which the replications do not totally suit the originals, that is, they do not ring totally true when compared. And that may be because the author (that is, I) did not feel like letting go of a particularly phrased original image considered dear. The long poem titled "The Space of Night" also was originally conceived and written in English. It presents a text apparently written in an alternate state of language awareness. Certain phrases simply cannot find suitable equivalents and so it was decided not to include the Spanish version of the poem. Another example of the difference in the expressive nature of the two languages can be found in the beginning of the "Ode to Sappho", where the Spanish uses the impersonal construction in a manner which is understood and felt to be actually personal ("Fue preciso conversar con las estrellas…"), whereas a more literal translation of that line ("It was necessary for me to converse with the stars…") would lose all its lyrical appeal.

There are both traditions and what I will call atmospheres in a culture. Language, in turn, responds to these human and social phenomena. In Spanish, for instance, words tend lyrically to cluster in a way they do much less in English; there is something cohesive about their sound that brings them together; they can elide as they do not in English. And so the rhythms of the two languages are different. English abounds in monosyllables while Spanish frequents longer words and longer phrases.

In poetry, when it comes to rhyme, either intended or not, Spanish is quite content with assonance or vowel-rhyme while English never was. And alliteration does not weaken the Spanish line as it seems to do in English. In the use of alliteration English takes a risk, as I did when I wrote in the poem "Ashes of the Dead": you cannot wed the waves or win the war. These object-details are crucial in the exercise of poetry translation which is ultimately a sort of transcription. But for example, the transcription of a musical composition for the violin into one for the violoncello is something else, because although it may involve different instruments, and perhaps modalities, like Cesar Franck´s famous Sonata, it happens in the same language. Not so with poetry, where the success of the work depends on two equally fortuitous factors: the ability of the translator and the adaptability of the poem. Some translators can translate some poems better than other translators and other poems.

The following pairs of poems hopefully will not turn out as tedious as twice-told tales (no reference to Hawthorne intended). They have the safeguard of consisting of one in English, the other in Spanish, so that they are not the same; they do not consist of repetitions. And let me say a word about myself. What is it, finally, about poetry, that makes me dedicated to it in all ways imaginable? We can try to write poetry, idealize it, even mythologize it, but ultimately it is, as all things human, something earthbound. And as such it allows me to think and feel and say whatever flows through my brain and the rest of my nervous system. It provides me with a view of life and of the world like nothing else. I, an ambilingual poet? Such an anomaly. As a friend of mine once put it: "You´ve sort of created your own literary path". (Which, I might add, has cost me the attention of many a publisher.)

Sometimes consciously, other times unconsciously, I´ve taken something from each culture when I write. Yet I never mix the two languages, I never indulge in code-switching, even though the social milieu is rife with it. Regardless of how much has melded in certain areas, such as science, technology, economics and politics (mostly generated by the English of powerful nations), regardless of the vaunted and rather execrable globalization pervading the air breathed by weak, fashionable individuals in the Third World, the deep consistency of authentic culture continues to resist contamination. And thus the vital nature of individual languages which thrives in literature and especially in poetry, with its particularities of sound and its complexities of meaning, manages to keep its own integrity.

This is exactly what I seek in my poetry, no matter the language in which I write.

Miguel Gonzalez-Gerth
December 15, 2006

Horse Latitudes is a name given to the region 30° either side of the Equator, where subsiding dry air and high pressure results in weak winds and confused seas. Tradition states that sailors gave this region the name *horse latitudes* because ships traveling to the New World sometimes stalled in the calm waters and, fearful of running out of food and water, crews were forced to throw their horses overboard to save on provisions.

CENIZAS DE LOS MUERTOS

ASHES OF THE DEAD

CENIZAS DE LOS MUERTOS

Cuando el sol está yéndose hacia el sur
en el otoño y hundiéndose cada vez más
en el cielo ártico, los esquimales de Iglulik
juegan con hilo formando una malla con
objeto de atraparlo e impedir así
su desaparición.
J.G. Frazer, La rama dorada

Cuando después de haber soltado el más hondo
lamento de la soledad uno reaparece,
semejante fantasma probablemente asumirá
el aura de un vidente. Pues lo que ve
no es aquello de que la gente habla.
Su relato es algo que las palabras mienten.

¿Qué fin tienen las cosas que decimos?

¿Son las palomas de la Piazza San Marco
las mismas que las de Trafalgar Square?
En algún sitio yace la respuesta y su verdad
trasciende todo espacio con límites abiertos.
La medida del amor intenta restaurar
el cuerpo ha tanto desollado.
Hay que robar al tiempo muy piadosamente,
llámese reliquia o como quiera,
y celebrar dicho prodigio con ritos de primavera,
y aunque remozado, por derecho de conquista, poseído:
lascivia del espíritu ("A ti, mar nuestro, unidos
en prueba de dominio verdadero y permanente").

De nuevo diestra lucha ha de librarse contra
un enemigo peligroso aunque en derrota,
y con viril piedra recordarse la victoria

ASHES OF THE DEAD

> *When the sun is going southward in the Autumn*
> *and sinking lower and lower in the Arctic sky,*
> *the Esquimaux of Iglulik play the game of cat's*
> *cradle in order to catch him in the meshes of the*
> *string and so prevent his disappearance.*
> J.G. Frazer, The Golden Bough

When having cried the deeper cry of loneliness
one reappears, such revenant is likely to assume
the aura of a seer. For what he sees
is not what people speak about, his
is a narrative which words betray.

What is the purpose of the things we say?

Are the pigeons in the Piazza San Marco
the same as those around Trafalgar Square?
Somewhere the answer lies and with its truth
transcends all space so openly confined.
The measure of our love tries to restore
a flesh torn off with iron long ago.
The pious theft must be achieved from time,
call it a saintly relic, call it what you will,
and celebrate the wonder with the rites of spring,
refurbished yet, by right of conquest, owned:
the spirit's lust ("We wed thee, oh our sea,
in proof of true and permanent dominion").

The skillful battle must again be fought
against an enemy in flight but always dangerous
and victory commemorated with a virile stone

("La patria cuenta con que cada hombre haga
su parte; gracias a Dios yo hice la mía").

¿Qué fin tienen las cosas que decimos?

Las decimos como un cebo, un juego de sonoros hilos
para atrapar al sol que no puede atraparse.
No hay forma cierta de unirse con las olas
o de ganar la guerra: hablar no es realidad, es arte.
En algún sitio todo lo ya dicho se deshace
cual columbario que de pronto queda abierto,
de donde las palabras, palomas que anidaron mucho tiempo,
las santas urnas rompen y aleteando escapan.

Traducción de Aurelio Asiain

("Your country counts on every man doing
his part, thank God I have done mine").

What is the purpose of the things we say?

We say them as a lure, a cat's cradle of sound
to catch the sunlight that will not be caught.
There is no way to really wed the waves or
win the war, to speak is not reality but art.
Somewhere the whole array of statements falls apart,
a columbarium rendered suddenly agape
where words, like doves that having nested much too long,
now break the holy urns and, fluttering, escape.

LA CARA DEL ESPEJO
A Octavio Paz

No hay nadie allí
y sin embargo creemos entrever
un mundo de entidades
que explicarían un contenido en el vacío
un abecedario de apariencias
un conato de conformación
de inconsecuentes congéneres cautivos

antropoide atado / adán atirantado / ángel ardiente
belleza que se vuelve belcebú
crisálida de la quimera
chamuco / chulapo / chocarrero
desilusión / delirio / doppelgänger
¿es el espejo falsedad
en que se abre el abanico de la realidad?
engendro erótico / envidia / envilecimiento / enojo
ficción / figuración y fingimiento
gorgona de gloria gorgotera
halo sin santo (aquí = allí)
ilusión (hija del yo) / ícaro ahogado
judas jabberwocki
cairos y cronos
lacrima christi logarítmica y liliputiense
llave que abre pero que no cierra.
maelstrón de melusina
nada que nada en la nada
ñiquiñaque ñoño
orfeo orante / orangután orondo
pitecántropo erigiéndose
¿quo vadis quantum brutus?
rêverie du revenant
simulacros simultáneos
tabula rasa (allí = aquí)

THE MIRROR'S FACE
For Octavio Paz

There is no one there,
and yet we think we see
a world of entities
that would explain a content in a void
an alphabet of images denoting
conformations of beleaguered sights.

ape a-hobble / Adam ribboned / angel aflame
beauty's being Beelzebub
chimera's chrysalis
dream / delusion / doppelgänger
is the mirror the reality
in which everything
displays its falsehood?
erotic elf / everyman's envy
fiction / figment / fragment
ghost or glorified gorgon
hallucination (here = there)
I (eye looking for illusion) / Icarus drowning
jabberwocky judas
kairos and kronos
lilliputian logarithmic lacrima christi

Melusina's maelstrom
nothing needing nothingness

Orpheus singing
pithecanthropus erecting
quo vadis, Brutus?
revenants's revery
simultaneous simulacra
tabula rasa (there = here)

utopía
variación del ojo antojo
x / exquisita equis
yo y también tú =
zurdería del cero

y el impulso continúa
el esfuerzo por sobrepasar
por penetrar (¡oh penetración!)
el velo celestial
el himen de cristal
por perturbar la materia debajo de la espira
con cincel o con espada
cortar la curva sólida de geometría
de libre habilidad hasta matar
hasta los huesos subyacentes en cavernas sombrías
inexistentes carapachos tan sólo imaginados
que se desvanecen
hasta que la polla / pluma / pene / pincel

que pisa la página
sucumbe a los sentidos hondamente quebrantados
de la incapacidad estéril
preludio del silencio que presagia
la infinita soledad
en un revés de misa negra
que luego recomienza la lúgubre epopeya
dentro del tres veces insondable
laberinto loco del pensamiento palabreado
allí en el espejo
donde no se encuentra / nadie

utopia
vision's variation's vagary
wraith / will-o'-the-wisp
x exquisite x
you and also I =
zero

and the urge goes on,
the effort to transcend,
to penetrate (oh penetration!)
behind the veil of glass,
the crystal hymen
to stir the staple underneath the steeple
with chisel and with sword
to carve the curve of solid geometry,
of unconventional creative skill and kill
until the bones in darkening caves,
the nonexistent shells only imagined
wear away,
until the pecker-penis-pencil-pen
that prances on the page
succumbs to crumbling senses
of barren incapacity,
of incredulity,
the prelude to the silence that portends
the infinite aloneness
like a reversal of Black Mass
renewing the lugubrious epopee
within a thrice abysmal,
zany labyrinth of worded thought
there in the mirror
where there is / no one

EL OTRO LADO DEL MAPA

El Atlántico era su océano.
El Mediterráneo era su mar.
Otras extensiones de agua:
el Lago de Ginebra, el Ródano,
el Río de la Plata.
Hoy, mientras contemplo el azul Pacífico,
sobre el cual voló dos veces,
pienso en Borges.
Pienso en todas las palabras:
las que me dijo a mí
y las que yo podría haber dicho.

Como el agua, las palabras fluyen
y, cuando sopla el viento,
forman olas, remansos, remolinos. Y desaparecen.
Quizá besen las riberas de la realidad
en las remotas bahías del tiempo,
llevando sus crestas consumadas
de ilusión fría
a romperse sobre la arena cálida.

Esas cabrillas
sabe usted, Borges,
esas pequeñas olas dóciles, cuya espuma
juega con los laberintos de la luz,
la luz vista y no vista,
constantemente vuelven
con el vaivén de la marea,
mojando el vidrio requemado
hasta que refleja la redondez del cielo,
el universo que se pierde
más allá de donde alcanza el pensamiento,
nómade inquieto en el espacio infinito.

THE OTHER SIDE OF THE MAP

The Atlantic was his ocean.
The Mediterranean was his sea.
Other bodies of water:
Lake Leman and the Rhône, the River Plate.
Now, as I look out over the blue Pacific,
over which he jetted twice,
I think of Borges.
I think of all the words:
those he said to me and those I could have said.

Like water, the words flow
and, as the winds blow,
they form waves and eddies. They disappear,
perhaps they lap at the shores of reality
in the bays of time,
bringing their consummate crests
of cold illusion
to break upon the heated sand.

Those whitecaps,
you know, Borges,
those docile little waves, whose foam
plays with the labyrinths of light,
seen and unseen light,
keep returning
with the motion of the tide,
wetting the sunburnt glass
till it reflects the total roundness of the sky,
the universe that strays
beyond the reach of mind,
a restless nomad in the realm of space.

Una bala de cañón de hace doscientos años
aún silba su canción fatal
al pasar volando.
Estoy sentado en la cubierta de un barco
cuya historia ha sido reducida,
de la firma de tratados importantes
al viaje de comunes y corrientes.

Miro fijamente el mar, un mapa
detrás del cual se ha ido acumulando
un fértil polvo
que mi pensamiento surca
lentamente como una proa.
Y el azul Pacífico
devuelve la mirada, acaso incrédulo
del cerco horizontal
que es el trasfondo de mis ojos.
Siento un suave movimiento
adormeciendo mis pasiones
sin alterar la vista,
la configuración imprecisa
de calladas, exuberantes, misteriosas islas
que navegan a mi lado.
Todo se hace con espejos, se me ha dicho,
salvo que Caín y Abel…
Nuestras palabras son como el azogue
de las estratagemas.
Borges, ¿está usted por allí también,
como en esa otra densa y nítida Babel?

A cannon ball two hundred years of age
still sings its fatal song
as it flew past.
I sit on the deck of a ship
whose history has been reduced
from the signing of great treaties
to the cruising of ordinary folks.

I stare at the sea. It is a map
behind which fertile dust has gathered
for my thought to plow as slowly as this prow.
And the blue Pacific
stares back at me, seemingly
incredulous of the horizon's rim that lies
behind my eyes.
There is a gentle sway
that lulls my passions
and yet does not affect the view,
the imprecise configuration
of the quiet, lush, mysterious islands
sailing by.
It is all done with mirrors, I am told,
except that Cain and Abel...
Our words are but the quicksilver of stratagems.
Borges, are you there too, as in that other Babel?

DESPERTAR

a la memoria de Betty

Ayer las flores eran todas frágiles.
Hasta el azafrán rebosó su belleza
sólo para perderla en inútiles remordimientos.
Al huir de todos los extraños,
no quería yo descubrir lo vulnerable
en todo lo que mi amor reclamaba.

Si alguna vez te negué,
ya no te niego ahora.
Un crucifijo emerge
rasgando las sombras
como un rayo ante mis ojos.

Cuando era niño y quizá por ser niño,
nadie me advirtió el peligro de los narcisos.
Y hoy que la primavera transforma
lo oscuro en brillantes acuarelas verdes,
apresurado me escondo en una zona gris
porque los lirios y los tulipanes
florecen bajo el sol.

Tus manos están vivas
en el musgo sensual,
en el lento vivir de las encinas,
en el sentido crepuscular de los helechos.

La brisa que toca el aire
es tu boca que besa al tocar,
y puedo dibujar tus cabellos
que flotan por oscuros subterráneos.
Ya no negada,

AWAKENING

In Betty's memory

Yesterday flowers were everywhere fragile.
Even the crocuses readied their beauty
only to waste it on useless remorse.
As I evaded the welcome of strangers,
I feared to discover the heel of Achilles
in everything claiming my love.

If ever I denied you,
I don't deny you now.
Rending the twilight,
a crucifix appears
as lightning in my eyes.

When I was a child,
perhaps because I was a boy,
nobody warned me of the danger of daffodils.
And now, as Spring goes about
replacing browns with joyous greens
and watercolors,
I hurry to hide on a neutral estate
when irises and tulips blossom in the sun.

Your hands are alive
in the softness of mosses,
in the sweet life of live oaks,
in the felt dusk of ferns.

Your mouth is a breeze
now touching the air.
Now kissing that touch,
I imagine your hair
flowing through subterranean landscapes.
No longer denied,

ya no negándote,
como el viento al levantarse somos
sólo uno en graníticas columnas.

Hace ya tiempo sentimos el amanecer
como un relámpago en los tímidos cristales
y compartimos un sinnúmero de cosas,
cuando el fuego aún latía en nuestras venas
y luego se escapaba como un ave temerosa.

Mi sangre y tu sangre eran
una sola llama y una sola furia.
Tus estrellas y las mías
se hundían en sueños profundísimos.
Mis ojos y tus ojos
ensombrecieron incontables horizontes.

El viento cantó por su camino
hasta llegar al fondo de la casa.
Las voces de los bosques
impulsaron mis andanzas juveniles.

Pero hubo alas que desde sitios lejanos
volaron hacia tu canción secreta.

La vida se fue ya para siempre,
como un enorme precipicio
causado por un grano de arena.
No podrá Cristo negarme
el judas de su perdón.
Tu sangre corre por mi sangre
hacia limítrofes sombras,
lunas crepusculares,
y llega por fin al origen
de mi lengua muda.

no longer denying,
we rise like the wind
in columns of granite
and are solid together.

Ages ago the dawn was seen only
as a flash on bashful windowpanes.
We shared so many things,
as time ticked by in our primal impulses
and then flew away with the frightened birds.

My blood and your blood
shared a flame and a fury.
Your stars and my stars
nestled deeply in dreams.
My eyes and your eyes
darkened countless horizons.

The wind chimed its way to the back of the house.
Voices from wildwoods
urged my youthful wandering.

Wings from distant places
wandered to your secret song.

We have to concede that life has changed forever,
like an enormous precipice
shifted by a grain of sand.
Christ can no longer deny
the Judas of my forgiveness.
Your blood in my blood flows
to the limits of sunsetting shadows
and reaches the birth of my muted tongue.

Tu fantasma permanece en el umbral.
Tu presencia no es ni retorno
ni señal de haberte ido.
Tus dedos trascienden delicados
las redes del quehacer terrestre,
mientras el fulgor de una luz naciente
abrillanta la corteza de la eternidad.

Frente al mar que mi vista alcanza
en súbitas ráfagas, la esencia insiste en despertar.
Los delfines del deseo
cantan en torno a un remolino,
más allá del tiempo y las mareas.
Y en una cuna de esplendor
todo se arrastra hacia el milagro.

Una piedra circular se ha apartado rodando.
Tú te has transfigurado
y tu corazón ha fundido al mío en cenizas.
El sol, como siempre, ascenderá al cenit
y crucificará otra vez al día.
Mas toda resurrección será lavada
por la lluvia primeriza.
La lluvia suena desde los cristales lúcidos.

Su toque suave acaricia la luz de la alborada.
Inocentes, los capullos otra vez florecen,
distraídos del peligro inmanente.

Mi reverencia cata la conmoción
de una abandonada eucaristía
en la bruma de cielos trágicamente perdidos.
Y miro con ojos ciegos
el fuego de la creación
en cuya gloria el mundo se recobra.

Traducción de Miriam Balboa Echeverría

You stand at the door like a ghost.
Your presence is neither return
nor the hint of a final departure.
Your fingers casually transcend
the patterns of earthly adventure,
as the splendor of a newborn light
tempers the surface of eternity.

The essence of being insists on awakening
with battering squalls
at the sea of my sight,
and the dolphins of desire chant
around a maelstrom beyond time and tide.
While in a cradle of radiance
everything is drawn into the miracle.

A circular rock has been rolled away.
You have achieved transfiguration.
My heart has been branded by your heart to ashes.
When, as always, the sun has reached its noon,
it will again have crucified the day.
But the early rain
has already washed its resurrection.
The sound of rain comes from emboldened glass.
The feel of rain is gentle,
stroking the light of dawn,
and flowers again blossom in their innocence,
forgetful of the risk in creature ways.

My reverence can taste the ferment
of a Eucharist abandoned
in the haze of lost and tragic skies,
and I can see with stricken eyes
the fire of creation
as the world is recovered by its glory.

NEWTON

No hay necesidad de rebuscar
en las ondas del aire y de la luz
para saber que el color y la música
que fluyen de mi oscuro pensamiento
apagado en tonos muy menores,
cuya densidad hace trizas la esperanza
y toda aproximación hacia el contento,
salvo esta solitud tan rústica
que me sorprende
con su hospitalidad modesta y reluciente:
revelan una tenaz conservación
sentimental de la materia,
de otra suerte escondida.
Podrán caer manzanas,
mas su majestad nunca desaparece.

NEWTON

One does not need to search
the waves of air and light
to realize the color and the music
emanating from the darkness of the mind
muffled by minor tones,
whose density shreds every hope,
every movement toward gladness
except this rustic solitude
that startles me
with its bright, modest hospitality:
reveal an unrelenting conservation
of sentimental matter
otherwise concealed.
Though apples fall,
their majesty never disappears.

REMORDIMIENTO

Híbrida timidez.
Un estremecimiento de gorriones que anuncia
un día desleído y desvencijado
y, sin embargo, con claridad convencional
de inhibiciones ya marchitas.

En tales ocasiones me valgo
de un rápido remordimiento
que envuelve los sentidos en una tenue gasa
con pliegues de recuerdo y olvido,
un acertijo de palabras tontas.
Y después de lentas horas melancólicas,
cuando el cansancio del ambiente
cede a la fuerza heroica de los objetos,
confundidos todos por el imán del verano,
una cigarra dispara su catedral acústica
en un crescendo más fuerte del que se esperaba,
tan agradable que alcanza alturas delirantes.
Esta es una evanescencia ajena a mi conciencia.
Absurdas reverberaciones.
Nadie se escapa de su espacio profético
en los sueños.

SEPTEMBER

To be done with September.
I can't bear it's delights.
I can't stand all the warmth
of the sounds and the sights.

To be done with September.
Let the anguish return.
Let the dankness of Autumn
quench the memories that burn.

To be done with September,
with July and with August.
Let the wind sweep the whispers
with its painfully raw gust.

To be done with September
and its fairytale meadows,
with its wide awake kisses
and its sunlighted shadows.

OTOÑO

"Señor, ya es hora. El verano ha sido
demasiado", dice Rilke.
La lluvia de anoche y de esta madrugada
ha cambiado el aspecto de la vida,
se ha filtrado por los intersticios,
se ha colado por la sustancia de las cosas.

Tiempo en los ojos,
mojado el mundo, se desvanecen los sueños
lavados por la leve claridad del cielo.
Son imaginables otra vez,
después de meses de sequía,
los ríos profundos con rocas sumergidas,
mares agitados por el voluble viento,
nubes horizontales y apagadas,
hasta gigantes lápidas de hielo.

El cielo encapuchado amenaza sombrío,
y los coágulos blancos
de líquido fertilizante y el aroma rosáceo
vivifican con su espanto
el piafar de las bestias en la caballeriza
del nostálgico año de mi señorío.

AUTUMN

"Lord, it is time. The Summer was too long,"
said Rilke.
Last night's and this morning's rains
have changed the look of things.
They have filtered through their narrow apertures.
They have seeped into their deepest substance.

Time in one's eyes,
the world now wet, dreams vanish,
washed away by the sky's early brilliance.
Once again imaginable,
after months of drought,
are rivers deep with sunken boulders,
seas stirred up by fickle winds,
dark, horizontal clouds,
even gigantic sheets of ice.

The hooded sky somberly threatens,
and white clots
of fertilizing liquids and rosy fragrances,
with their wonder, vivify
the stamping of beasts in the stable
of this nostalgic time that is my lordship.

NAUFRAGIO DE SIRENAS

SHIPWRECK WITH MERMAIDS

DESDE UNA VENTANA

Inspirada en una litografía de
Yves Ganne

Una mujer contempla un mar antiguo.
No es algo prehistórico
sino un sentimiento casi eterno.
Una bahía con barcos cuyas velas
pespuntean la tarde.
Un horizonte que se reconoce a sí mismo
en la mano gentil que lo saluda.
¿Bienvenida o despedida?

El horizonte se refleja en la bahía
más allá de donde los barcos con sus velas
pespuntean la tarde.
La mujer eres tú,
como ya se había prefigurado.
Indiferente no, cautelosa cual reciente
miras hacia un exterior que no es ajeno,
un mar horizontal que ya conoces
porque una vez lo recibiste entero.

Y ahora, desde una ventana,
casi detrás de una cortina,
un velo sigiloso,
atisbas aquello que representa lo perdido
y lo que aún queda por venir;
la vida que desespera a las gaviotas,
las olas de espuma que ligeras
se rompen en la playa,
y, por la noche, después de haber mirado,
después de haber enviado aquel saludo
silencioso,
la eternidad de un firmamento marinero

WINDOW VIEW

After a color lithograph by
Yves Ganne

A woman gazes at an ancient sea.
The scene does not evoke prehistory
but a feeling near eternity.
A bay with boats whose sails
backstitch the afternoon.
A horizon that can see itself
in a gentle hand that waves to it.
Is it a greeting or a farewell?

The horizon is reflected in the bay
beyond the boats whose sails
backstitch the afternoon.
The woman being you,
as one might have foreseen,
is not aloof and yet, with recent cautiousness
looks out at something quite familiar:
a horizontal sea you recognize,
which once upon a time
you welcomed whole.

Now, from the vantage of a window view,
almost hidden by a curtain,
a veil of caution,
perhaps you look for what you lost
and what is yet to come:
a life that drives the seagulls mad,
the frothy waves that quickly break
upon the beach.
And in the night, after having scrutinized,
after having waved your hand
ever so silently, you feel
the timelessness of seaborne skies

en que los astros cumplen su función
por fin no eterna pero sí grandiosa.

De dentro afuera miras,
de fuera adentro sientes.
El velo, la cortina apenas delimita
la tensión, la frágil intención
de tu mirada.
¿Qué miras? ¿Qué buscas en un término
de lejanía que no distingue nadie,
en un tramo de mar que se quedó allá lejos,
en los años locos del crepúsculo?

Yo creo, como poeta casi detective,
con la certeza de un hombre que confía
en sus firmes intenciones,
en sus inventos de vana analogía,
opino, por decir al fin ya casi nada,
que buscas lo que ya buscaste entonces,
lo que buscaste en aquel tiempo irresoluto y vago,
más allá de las seguridades prometidas.
Buscas lo mismo, amor mío, mirando sólo,
atisbas desde lejos, desde la protección
de tu ventana lo que antes saludaste
ingenuamente,
jugando tus pies con las espumas,
tus manos con las olas,
tus ojos con el verde azul de la osadía.

Buscas lo mismo cautelosamente,
detrás del velo protector de la cortina,
porque la vida ha sido y ha pasado,
y sólo así sabemos lo que pasa,

where stars fulfill their mystery,
ultimately not quite eternal
yet certainly magnificent.

From inside outwardly you look.
From outside inwardly you feel.
The veil, the curtain barely lines
the tension, the delicate intention
of your gaze.
What are you looking for?
What do you seek in such a stretch
of distance which no one can define,
in such a patch of sea left far behind,
in the crazy age of twilight?

I do believe,
as poet acting as detective,
with the certainty of one
who trusts his firm impressions,
inventions based on vain analogies,
I think (and this is saying almost nothing)
that you are seeking what you sought before,
in that vague and vacillating time
beyond all promised certainties.
You seek the same, my love, but from afar.
From far away, from the protection
of your window view, you still remember
what you grasped with utter innocence:
your feet playing with the froth,
your hands playing with the waves,
your eyes playing with the dare
of blue-green.
And now you wish the same but cautiously,
behind the curtain's guard, the veil,
because your life was not to temporize.

sólo así sabemos lo que es vida.
Y, sin embargo, aun así queremos recibir
y luego despedir
lo que sólo se vive en la mirada.

Since one can only know life having lived,
since one can only know life having seen,
we wish to greet and then to leave
what only can be lived within our eyes.

PUERTO

Luces en el puerto. Se estremecen los sentidos
ávidos de lejanía.
Hace ya tanto tiempo
que no he visitado este sitio
a la vez abstracto y concreto,
donde ahora se mezclan la memoria y los deseos
en un apogeo candente de sonrisas tristes.

El mar latente es un muelle de olas lisas.
De noche, en este momento preciso,
el cielo se acerca a la tierra
en un vaivén recíproco de sombra y luz.
Y en lo alto
un azul que se ha tornado claroscuro
reposa como un ancho terciopelo
desteñido por la sal del tiempo.

Junto al malecón los barcos se mecen silenciosos.
Su silencio, junto con su realidad viajera,
me obliga a navegar por rutas nuevas,
impensadas, mas no por eso no queridas.
Memoria y deseo,
chispas de la vida que me incitan a buscar
muy dentro de la oscuridad del mundo
las luces en el puerto.

HARBOR

Lights along the harbor.
My senses are ashiver, covetous of distance.
It's been so long since I have visited this place
as I once did.
A place that is both abstract and concrete,
where now my memory and my desire mesh
in a burning culmination of sorrowful smiles.

The latent sea. A pier by mulling waves.
At night and at this moment
the earth appears to touch the sky
in a mutual, silent sway of shadow and light.
Up high,
a blue that has become both dark and bright
drapes like a velvet cloth
discolored by the salt of time.

At the docks, boats silently rock.
Their silence, together with their fact of sail,
impels me into virgin routes,
previously unthought and yet not unappealing.
Memory and desire,
living sparks that urged me here to seek,
within the darkness of the world,
this harbor and its lights.

OLA

Nace la ola misteriosamente.
Es agua y también es viento.
Es movimiento.

El aire que la forma algo le quita.
El cuenco que la informa la ciñe y la limita.

Pero la ola surge y con su afán alcanza
la arena de la playa.

Ahora se aleja
de la desesperada sed del día.
Entonces se acerca
al hambre insaciable de la noche.

¿De dónde habrán venido aquellas gotas,
aquel granizo cálido
que se fulge con temblor de cielo?

Y ¿dónde habrá encontrado aquella sal
que muerde el mapa que es la piel
de lo irredento?

¿Qué redondez la habrá impregnado
para que lleve en derredor del mundo
su dócil tempestad de amor viajero?

Las nubes sacrifican la visión profunda
del mar perfecto.
Y las estrellas como peces cruzan
el espacio que despacio inunda
el líquido de su secreto.

WAVE

The wave is born mysteriously.
It's made of wind and water.
And it has movement.

The air that forms it takes something from it.
The cradle that informs it hugs it and restricts it.

But the wave swells and in its eagerness
it breaks upon the sand along the beach.

Now it moves away
from the desperate thirst of day.
Then it returns to approach
the insatiable hunger of night.

Where did those drops come from,
those warm hailstones
that glisten with the tremor of the sky?

And where did it find that salt
that bites the map that is the skin
of all that's living unredeemed?

What roundness could have filled it
so it can carry all around the earth
the docile tempest of its wayward love?

The clouds can come to sacrifice
the profound vision of the perfect sea.
And the stars like fishes swim across
a downward space being slowly filled
by a liquid from its secret maze.

BAHIA

La noche en su litoral
separa las luces de las sombras
y juega con el agua maciza,
ahora clara, ahora oscura,
a veces rala, a veces honda.

El agua tiene vocación de sirena
y sobre la playa se desparrama.
Pero la noche sabe que los peces
sin su cola no son nada.

El agua deja su impronta
en la arena desolada.
Deja su huella celeste
de cielo que se desgaja.
Pero la noche se calla.

La noche traza una curva
en la bahía de la distancia.
Separa la luz de la sombra
y el canto de la caracola.

BAY

At the shoreline the night separates
the lights from the shadows
and plays with the firmer waters,
now clear, now dark,
sometimes deep, sometimes shallow.

The water wants to be a mermaid
and stretches out over the beach.
But the night happens to know
that fish without a tail can't swim.

The water can leave its mark
on the lonely sand.
It leaves a heavenly mark
of a sky that fell to earth.
But the night says not a word.

The night traces a curve
in the bay of the far along,
separating light from shadow
and the seashell from its song.

BESOS DE SIRENA

Han pasado por la calle de mi olvido
innumerables besos.

Los pocos que recuerdo
han sido besos de sirena y ésos
solamente los he visto.

Los he visto
con mis ojos fustigados por el sueño.
Y hambre he sentido,
hambre en los huesos.

Esos besos de sirena me han dejado
un resquemor lejano y dolorido.
Y donde los he visto no ha sido
junto al mar resplandeciente y rezagado
sino en un pozo ya baldeado e intranquilo,
entre las aguas desteñidas por el frío.

No me he atrevido
a rozar con mis labios esos besos.
Pero desesperadamente los recuerdo
porque los he visto.

SIREN KISSES

On the street of my forgetting
many kisses I have passed.

The few I can remember
have been siren kisses.
And those I have only seen.

I have seen them with my eyes
lashed by sleeplessness.
And then I have felt hunger,
hunger in my bones.

Those siren kisses have left me
distantly and soulfully forlorn.
Yet where I've seen them has not been
by the languid and resplendent sea
but in a well restless and awash,
amid its water discolored by the cold.

I have not dared
to graze those kisses with my lips.
And yet I recall them very well
because I've seen them.

DILACIÓN NOCTURNA

El mar trepida ondulante.
Dilación capilar de un ancla
en secreto.

Van cediendo los caireles
del viento.
Se siente un acercamiento ocular
de íntimas disecciones.

Y esgrimiendo incesante
sus áureos floretes
contra el crespón airoso del vacío,
la luz se va haciendo compacta
hasta esconderse
en una cajita de agujas como guiños.

La solución de sol y sal disuelve
los rencores del día.
Al fin la oscuridad con su mandoble
cercena toda elección ultramarina.

NOCTURNAL SLACK

The sea trepidates while rocking,
capillary dialation of a secret anchor.

The vehement curls of the wind
begin to taper.
One can feel the ocular approach
of intimate dissections.

And deftly wielding its golden blade
against the airy voile of the void,
light becomes slowly compact
until it hides
in a little box of needles much like winks.

The solution of sun and salt
dissolves the rancors of the day.
In the end darkness with its double axe
curtails all choice beyond the blue.

DESENCUENTRO

Si tus ojos me trajeron las honduras
de las aguas del mar,
de inmediato sospeché el peligro
de las altas mareas
y el naufragio seguro en la resaca.

Contemplé la ronda de delfines
que te acompañaba
y disfruté inexplicablemente
la angustia de morir ahogado
en la tempestad de tu mirada.

Quizá soñé
(soñando se vislumbran los deseos)
con descubrir
profundos secretos.
Quise hallar toda emoción
de que es capaz el alma.
Y mi albedrío
(genio varado en esta isla cotidiana)
pudo alcanzar de los relámpagos
la pertinaz distancia.

El ámbito del gozo se me abrió
como un hermoso iris de ilusiones.
Te acercaste entonces.
Hice un esfuerzo por echar el ancla.
Quise dar fondo como viejo buen marino.

Pero de largo nos pasamos
como dos veleros fantasmas.
Y por alto se pasaron
(en el insomnio de esta isla cotidiana)
tantas cosas impensadas.

MISCHANCE

Since your eyes brought me the depth of the sea
I perceived at once the danger
of high tides
and of the certain shipwreck at low ebb.

I beheld the round of dolphins
that came escorting you
and surprisingly enjoyed the dread of drowning
in the tempest of your gaze.

Perhaps I dreamed
(in dreams we discover our wishes)
I might discover unfathomable secrets.
I tried to find every emotion given to one's soul.
And by the power of sheer will
(my nature grounded on this ordinary island)
I managed to arrive at the determined distance
of the lightning.

The space of pleasure opened
like a lovely rainbow of illusions.
Then you approached.
I made an effort to cast anchor
like an old experienced sailor.

But we passed each other like two phantom ships.
And so
(in the sleeplessness of this ordinary island)
so many unexpected things
went on their ways.

NAUFRAGIO

Por el aire estriado,
como desde una hondonada
en que se petrifica el tiempo
– arrecife de coral desmoronado –
se escucha un ulular de voces lánguidas,
líquidas,
acuáticas,
lunáticas,
infundidas de un dolor indescriptible:
voces que se tornan casi mudas
cuando se oyen desaprensivamente:
aires conmovidos que revuelan con caídas alas
o más preciso es decir que con aletas:
peces vagos en vano reconocimiento
como espías que desearan delatarse:
diseminados flujos invisibles,
deleznables,
inasibles,
desleídos
en la ora lenta, ora rápida escritura
hecha de un rielante abecedario,
de un insondable y trágico extravío:
un llanto que fue canto y es sollozo,
que es muerte de esperanza o es suicidio
anunciado levemente en un ocaso
y en incierto conticinio perceptible,
cuando la luna luce sus lunares fríos,
cuando su luz plomiza cae a plomo
y ciertamente aquieta las mareas,
cuando por fin se extinguen seres
que antes se creyeron inmortales,
que ya en su moridura presintieron
que el universo muere astro por astro:
sirenas que naufragan en su noche última
y se arroban con las sombras de los cielos.

SHIPWRECK

In the fluted air
as from a ravine in which time is petrified
– a coral reef abraded –
one can hear the wail of languid voices,
liquid,
watery,
lunary,
infused with indescribable pain:
voices that become almost soundless
when one does not expect them,
like a pathetic air fluttering with fallen wings
or more precisely fins:
a weeping that resembles the flickering of fish
in their exhausted movement in the deep:
vague fish in useless exploration,
like spies that wish to be denounced:
scattered and invisible fluidity,
slippery,
unseizable,
deliquescent in the now slower, now quicker scripture
made of a shining alphabet,
of a profound and tragic aberration:
a cry that was a song and now a weeping,
that is the death of hope or suicide
once barely uttered in a twilight
or an uncertain yet conspicuous dead of night,
when the moon displays her frigid beauty spots,
when her leaden light falls perpendicular
and surely lulls the tides,
when finally creatures are extinguished
who had thought themselves immortal,
and in their dying found
that the universe dies one star after another:
mermaids who in their final night begin to drown
and are enraptured with shadows of the heavens.

REALIDAD DEL PRESENTE

Despierto. Estoy aun cerca del mar.
La bahía traza su arco azul
de media luna centelleante.
El faro duerme. Ha dormido muchos años,
desde que nuevas señales guían
el cauteloso virar de los timones.

Voy despertando y va cuajando
la imagen aleteante del presente.
Mis sentidos se afinan a la brisa
que me deja su frescura matutina.

Sigo mi despertar cual soñador embelesado
que sigue con sus ojos la fugaz estrella
que cae en el abismo de la nada
que es el todo del mirar.
Me desperezo con albricias
que me ofrece el día,
regalándome sus cantos y sonrisas.

Ya despierto totalmente, miro el mar.
Distingo entre tonalidades y volúmenes.
Las crestas de las olas blancas salvo
por un esquivo instante,
un vuelco atlético que me produce
la ilusión un tanto musical
de ignotas y rebeldes juventudes.

El sol toca sus dianas en oriente.
Convierte el horizonte en bandera tricolor.
Unos pelícanos vuelan cerca de la playa
y hacen de las aguas claras un espejo
con el reflejo de sus alas.

REALITY OF THE PRESENT

I wake. I'm near the sea.
The bay draws a blue arc,
a sparkling half moon.
The lighthouse sleeps.
It's been asleep for years,
since recent signals guide
the cautious turning of the helms.

I begin waking, and the fluttering image
of the present starts to jell.
My senses tune in to the breeze
that brings to me its morning cool.

I follow my waking like a dreamer charmed
whose eyes follow a star
that falls into the void that is all eyes.
I wake up with delight,
delight I offer to the day,
charged as it is with songs and smiles.

I'm now awake. I look toward the sea
where I discern its hues and volumes.
For a mere blink, a near athletic tumble
creating in my soul an almost musical illusion
of forgotten, carefree youth,
I clear the crests of iridescent waves.

At last the sun sounds reveille.
Its clarion brings oriental colors
to the clouds.
Some pelicans fly closer to the beach
and turn translucent waters
into mirrors that reflect their wings.

Y la mañana embiste
y me viste de tristeza a la vez que de alegría.
El pasado es mi sueño, mas despierto estoy.

The morning charges like a bull.
It bathes me both in sadness and in joy.
The past is all a dream. I am awake.

THE SPACE OF NIGHT

THE SPACE OF NIGHT

conticinium aeternitatis
summum raptus est
            — Lucan

El conticinio casi ya pasando iba...
            — Sor Juana Inés de la Cruz

                        ... night
dwells and I contemplate the sight
that is not seeing, but the light
that is secretely kindled...
            — A. Crowley

        In the shining pupils of a cat
it is believed that all the night is gray.
And yet that is not so.
Inside the velvet hidden from the light
lie greens and blues and incredible golds,
singular in number and circular in sign,
with piercing flecks of violet hue.

Those eyes see life with regular strokes,
rays like ghosts with differing tones,
invisible colors no one can discern
as the white of the moon taunts the midnight sky.

By virtue of reflection we all see.
To beauty of refraction we are blind.
But all things turn to light
for quickness in their life,
though darkness is by far more soft
in its slow and shadowless retreat.
Light from on high traverses constant chance.

It gives consistency to space
and summons thought from utmost time,
mixing it all in a continuous snare
that's the survival of a lively dream.

Ruffled larks sing out their praise.
Mottled glimmers bolting like a precious stone
daze imagination turned to vision,
flickering and spinning to deep foliage
through a gauze of intangible stealth.

In the leopard night, avid in ambush,
after the padded step has stalked its last,
the universe appears intensely still,
quiet and vibrant with electric force
a silent and resplendent beast,
it purrs and barely undulates,
heaving its calm yet vivid breath.

We should imitate such wholesome rest,
such sheaf of springs so in repose.
We should flee from the sinister gadfly
buzzing in the boredom of the streets,
and finally hide in awesome revelation
where only pure liberty exists.
Space! Space! Infinite space
confined in its darkness.
The light of the moon gently invites
us to breathe the audible silence:
at the bottom of the sea, the rocky trees;
at the paling altitudes, the locks of fleece.

In what dimensions can we measure space
without the risk of canon weight?
Boundless or bound, the dazzle of extent
transcends the uniformity of mind

and the conformity of fantasy annuls.
It is a simple, cornerless beyond
where death no longer sadly smiles,
where everything is certain to return.
Even the vectors, victors over light,
preventing it from leveling creation
groping in the dark.

Everything moves until it finds its rest.
Everything nests as soon as it has found
the secret ring of days,
a filtering of fateful sparks,
predictions gathered from the streams of time
and offered to the wake of a seafaring moon,
so dour and pure
that, like a driven conch
or outrageous wraith in somber flight,
unleashes a decipherment of codes
coldly decanted by the threads of stars.

Meanwhile, in the land of those yet living,
the young girls flaunt beguiling limbs,
their nakedness an incandescent beam
of fiery, tantalizing flesh.

Let us proceed in silence and disdain
to hidden gardens of indolent relief,
to parks where sunshine does not burn,
where living makes an eddy and then swells
finally singing with triumphant voice,
like mermaids who have ultimately traced
the fickleness of sound to triton shells.

In the plummet of a whole abyss
the intermingled hearts of pain
secretely begin to fall apart,

and a benign existence is unveiled
as it approaches inconspicuous glades
hovered over by luxuriant shade.
Then solitude dethrones the watershed
of any wakeful rumination.

> Meanwhile, in the land of those yet living,
> acts are all subject to their consequence,
> appearances are what things used to be,
> and washed out dreams are still enshrined.

In the nebulous realm of oscillating dark,
made sentient by some brightly splintered sun,
the zodiac-light can dress in final garb
the horizontal posture of the dead,
enveloping in passion ages past
and crystallizing marble into shape.

The thicket's leaves continue trembling
in the gallery of such eternal being,
pictures and torsos scale the walls.
Landscape is not an image anymore
but land reflecting eyes that would escape.

In the space of this restful, feline night,
while a throbbing void reverberates,
your eyes and mine will catch the fire
distilling through the garret of the skies.
Upon the widened, lengthened, layered line,
the last horizon now beyond reprieve,
unnumbered lamps are overturned.
Reflected fields adhere to blooms.
Close, close your eyes! The blue is all too high!
And playing leapfrog on the Pleiades
the mass of light looks for the dawn.

Ah, the space of night shines more
than even that of day.
Every sound, however faint, can be perceived
as if all distance were totally resolved.

Every horrifying rap,
every telling crepitation
piercing the air with eager lance
becomes the convoluted object
of our living human fright.
The sensory diction of unerring tunes
allays the warning of the passing clouds.
Beyond, the visible invades the world
in waves that stimulate the skin of time.
Echoes evade the corners of the stars,
evoking beings possessed of bare
configurations of recall.
Soft chirps revive the sensibility
of mold, the prototype of crows
that mark the route of migratory flights
left tattersall on some forsaken map,
flights much too high for restful sleep
and much too low to manage dreams
which no one dared to visualize
a million years ago.

Here, in this leafy growth of green,
our bodies are transfigured now
and woven into fabric of the infinite
in a conspiracy of geometry and soul.
Such angles being swift as wings,
the hand that will caress you then
will be my happiness condemning wrongs.

In the space of this so welcome night,
this wooded glen of shaking leaves,

the feverish darlings of desire
will loose their sway and ruthless thirst.

> Meanwhile, in the land of those yet living,
> a past and perfect reason is adored,
> wars are compared to simple droughts
> and honesty gives way to mere façade.

The wheel of hours must be stopped.
We must repeal the barren laws.
We must repel the burgeoning assault
made by an army hoisting flags of smut.
We must remain concealed as by eclipse
and, tenants of the blue, stroll on the clouds,
convinced that in this primal state
lies our conclusive and perpetual hope.
As the duration of the conscious mind
keeps turning round an aura multiple and vast,
an incandescent register of willful acts,
the fulcrum whence a strike articulates
the luminous precision
of the clock of light,
the sundogs' howling that pervades
the just meridian of the basic day,
establishing in utter consonance
the hasty reaches of our grasp,
though causing memories of love to fade.
Like plumes of water, like a fragile rain,
the fluttering wish of a caress,
a glance of petals and of words,
is the lover's watching over the beloved.
And you will go, noble and unclothed,
on the tide of an unexpected daybreak.
You will leave me anchored in the bay of dawn
over which you will return in radiant dress.

Neither the scattered scudding clouds
nor the wind of shuttlecocks
can alter the harmonious strings
of heaven's harps.
Music can be heard, latent and warm,
the only hum from anguished keys
able to perform incipient chords
so graceful that they bend the breeze.

A trail of rancor now has disappeared.
Yet rivers vanish only in the sea.
The sea has drowned an echo of mirage,
and we can go no farther.
Here we lie
and ask our love to teach all hate to smile.
And from the tops of trees will be proclaimed
the impotence of the redundant world.
The honeycombs will welcome solitude
and, motionless, without a wince of fright,
we will embrace the cross of peace.

Meanwhile, in the land of those yet living,
a fleet of promises is fast approaching,
gifts of corruption are indeed forthcoming
and hideous idols worshiped as sublime.

In this tufted night of ancient space
the sky will make a prison overthrown,
an open casement set aflame,
a penitence of freedom to our souls.
And yet forever we will surely keep
the reticence and strength that mark our love.
The age of wool, of ivory the age,
the immanence of lamb and mastodon
roll down a road of molten wax.
And far behind, where everything has passed,

our eyes at last will slowly close.
A slight bloodthirsty flame will glow
within our dear beheaded time.
Birds larger than the winds
with beak and talon will dispute
a gnarled, gigantic birthing roost
left from the tempest-battered trees.
All that and even more will come
right after us.

        Meanwhile, in the land of those yet living,
        the waves of chance come crashing down,
        ominous vessels seek new ports
        and seabirds flee evils unknown.

In the hollows of the breezes' net
we will not look for our friends.
Life crumbles dolefully throughout,
and there is universal pain.
Must we resign ourselves to hecatomb?
Filth has just spoken the last word.
The trill of birds has slowly died,
while much revered ancestral vows
and immemorial writing slates
have quietly and humbly become dim.

Should we surrender to the cunning crowd?
We must persist upon the final strands
of human resolution in the wild.
For there are marvels still to be explored
and that which saves man from himself.
We must achieve an equidistant pose,
at once up close and yet afar.
We must resist the blows of greed
after unnumbered years adrift.
We must recover everything we lost.

Birds will adorn the sparkling wood.
Rocks will enjoy their subterreanean homes,
and we will thrive on the angelic points
of animal yet human thorns.
A griffin's grace will nestle in our breast,
then ignorant of miseries and crimes.

Meanwhile, in the land of those yet living,
intelligence is under house arrest.
What was a will became a destiny
and hunger colonizes every place.

All those we think that we have known
now live in some unnoticed town.
Life trickled out through tidy hair,
and ice will finish sculpting them.
As with the motion of all wanderers,
so move the most primordial plants
that modeled life since it occurred,
falling to earth, rising to sunlight,
navigating to ebullient waters
of millennial night,
until it deliquesced in the torrential
flood of time.
Yes, we will rest in perfect sleep,
in this green grange with trembling leaves.
In your dark eyes great jewels will converge
from fertile distances and incidental mines.
We will await whatever future holds
in murmurs sent from mangers far above,
where a terrestrial being was foretold
in tender yet exciting shudderings.
The wanton demon of delight
will finally arise within our tears.

Meanwhile, in the land of those yet living,
threatening trucks transport platoons,
strong, weak and rotten mean the same
and rains are nothing but delayed events.

Truth is a willow weeping by a lake.
We must not fear the dusty grove
where voices from the past can still be heard.
Let us assume the path to certain bliss
by entering this thicket's raptured calm.
Let us abandon rueful thought at once
as we are welcomed by the tempting mist.

To the frightening scream
that readies the dying
as they hide in the twilight,
either early or late,
our spirits are drawn
in astonishing colors,
in shades that defy any semblance of sense.
And the ultimate union
inherent in silence,
the deep quietude
pervaiding the air
is only the frame
in which phantoms appear.
A soul takes its hold,
like a remora of time,
fulfilling a settled
though now futile bond
that looks beyond disheveled barns
keeping the ample calendars of life.

In the very instant that precedes the dawn,
as the day breaks out into an icy flood,
like the dazzling flourish of the rainbow's jack

everything merges in a crown of light
like knives.

The glen absorbes us in its nupcial depth,
as the transit of Venus approaches its end.
Everything mingles in a darting strike.
a sudden thrust of transubstantial might.
The wane of the moon is the claw of a cat
carefully drawn in the space of night.

EN BUSCA DE LAS CALMAS ECUATORIALES

LOOKING FOR THE HORSE LATITUDES

INVITACIÓN

Astro de la mañana, Luzbel,
mi antiguo e infinito huésped.
Sigues a la oscuridad nocturna
con tu propia oscuridad secreta.

Por medio del hechizo, mas con sabiduría,
de un más allá hecho de notas cristalinas
truecas la vida santa
en un bosque hecho de tiempo.

No sé por qué te invoco,
endiablada linterna de espacio exhausto,
hábil tentador del ambicioso Fausto
quien, entre libros y crisoles transparentes,
fundió su alma con escoria y oro.

El tiempo alado es de Fortuna el dado.
Te llamo porque no tengo alternativa
hasta que el círculo se mude en cuadro.
Astro de la mañana, Luzbel,
mi huésped antiguo e infinito.

INVITATION

Star of the Morning, Lucifer,
my infinite and ancient guest.
You come following the dark of night,
bringing the darkness of a secret sense.

By means of sorcery yet with the wisdom
of a beyond performed in crystal notes,
you change a holy life
into a forest of time.

I do not know why I invoke you,
bedeviled lantern of exhausted space,
skillful tempter of ambitious Faust
who, amid transparent crucibles and books,
melted his soul with slag and gold.

Winged Time is Fortune's die.
I call you because I have no choice
until the circle turns into a square.
Star of the Morning, Lucifer,
my infinite and ancient guest.

ESCALERA

Por un caracol de despedida
allora per gli addii scala
las damas van descendiendo
rojo intenso negro
lento malva leve
como el espíritu de Giacomo Balla
barandal vuelta tras vuelta
de hierro cada balaustre
de mármol cada peldaño
y de encaje los sombreros
en escalones volados
sonrisas hilvanan miradas
enaguas de andares como agua
curvas transitan las curvas
curvas subieron y bajan
a tiempo llegarán al fondo
raíz de vida raíz de casa
cuántos pasos en declive
cuántos pisos en redondo
miradas pespuntan risas
desde la altura invisible
allora per gli addii scala
las damas han ido bajando
rojo intenso negro
lento malva leve
desde una nostalgia abúlica
las hemos imaginado

STAIRWAY

The ladies wave as they descend
the stairway in spiral
allora per gli addii scala
vivid red along with black
slow and light the mauve
like the spirit of Giacomo Balla
the railing turning and turning
each baluster made of iron
and every step made of marble
and all their hats of lace
along the flight of stairs
smiles basted to looks
skirts in a flowing gait
curves that move round the curves
curves went up and curves come down
soon they will reach the ground
root of life as well as the house
so many steps to go up as down
so many floors round and round
looks backstitch the ladies' laugh
coming from the hidden top
allora per gli addii scala
the ladies have now come down
vivid red along with black
slow and light the mauve
and from a languid wistfulness
we have imagined them

TRANSICIÓN

Como un deshielo en primavera
del cual pueden fluir nuestras vidas
después de haber estado encajonadas,
antes que el cajón antes de pino,
debe surgir un sentido de descanso
como el despertar de una crisálida,
una resurrección antes del alba,
antes de volver a la oscuridad
y después al día final, eterno y absoluto.

Cuando ya no dormimos ni soñamos,
cuando ya no morimos ni somos engañados,
entonces fluye la vida como fluye el agua,
cuando ya no fluye la sangre por las venas
sino que fluye más allá de lo que es sangre,
buscando nuevas cimas y nuevas latitudes
corre y vuela en alas nuevamente desplegadas
como corre el agua cuando deja de ser hielo
y se olvida de la tierra cual nube que se eleva,
lirio en llamas que se vuelve luz pascual,
pequeña mañana de tiempo derramado,
piedra que se vuelve pájaro y luego chispa,
jaula que se abre y después desaparece,
vuelo que de hielo con velas desplegadas
              confiere libertad.

TRANSITION

Like a thaw in Spring
from which our lives can flow
after having been boxed in,
before that other box once made of pine,
there must arise a feeling of surcease
like the awakening of a chrysalis,
an instant resurrection before dawn,
before returning to the dark and then
to the final, absolute, eternal day.

When we no longer sleep or dream,
when we no longer die or are deceived,
then life flows quietly as water flows,
when blood no longer flows inside the veins
but flows ahead beyond what mere blood is,
looking for newer latitudes and peaks
it runs and flies on newly sprouted wings
as water runs when it stops being ice
and then forgets the earth as climbing cloud,
a burning lily turned to paschal light,
a tiny morning of apportioned time,
stone that becomes bird and is a spark,
cage that is opened and then disappears,
flight that from ice with lifted sails
        awards release.

LO INDEFINIBLE

Esa emoción escrita oh
rodea la conmoción llamada yo.
El círculo verbal
revela y a la vez esconde,
la voz es un complejo cómplice
del crimen más sublime
crimen fuga
dádiva de vida
amar oh el vivir
vivir yo el amor
cualquiera es sólo el otro
ninguno es aquel otro
que va a morir tranquilo
como las alas de los pájaros
anidadas en la brisa
de su vuelo y de su sueño
en que sueña el cielo
indiferencia atroz del tiempo
horas en que el amar es todavía vivir
años en que el vivir deviene amor.

IN DEFINITION

That indefinite emotion written O
encircles the commotion known as I.
But verbs contrast and blend
together so to gather.
The voice is an accomplice
and on complicity depends.
To live, O, I love.
To love, O, I live.
Partners in the crime sublime
of revelation, of living, and of giving.
Otherwise a pack of lies,
where either is like other
and neither is another.
To kill is to collect and not to save.
To give is to survive the sowing.
To die is peaceful as the wings
of doves which, nestled in the breeze
of a mercurial flight,
will somehow, someday overtake the sun.
And indefinably,
in the meanness of our time,
to live is yet to love.

FANTASMA

Soy pescador de cristales.
Navego parsimoniosamente
conjurando imágenes de agrado,
evitando arrecifes de suicidio.

Estas metáforas sugieren mi trabajo,
el ronco oficio que he heredado
junto a linternas mecidas por el viento.
Y los mares que atravieso bajo los astros nublados,
entre el fragor de máquinas vencidas,
jamás serán, como lo eran, serenos.

Me voy por el mundo de luces quietas
y aguas entumecidas
hasta llegar, como remando se llega,
a las playas translúcidas hechas
de una holanda ya desvanecida.

GHOST

I am a fisher of crystals.
Prudently I sail,
conjuring pleasant images,
avoiding suicidal reefs.

Such metaphors suggest my work,
the coarse trade I've inherited
next to lanterns swayed by the wind.
And the seas which I traverse
under the cloudy stars,
amid the noise of vanquished engines,
will never be, as they once were, serene.

I sail through a world of quiet lights
and of surging waves,
and someday I will reach,
as by rowing one can reach,
translucent beaches made
of fine Dutch linen
that has already disappeared.

EN BUSCA DE LAS CALMAS ECUATORIALES

A partir del cuadro Rooms by the Sea
de Edward Hopper

Algo que no se ve preocupa
la elasticidad del pensamiento.
Las apariciones cotidianas
han sido totalmente exorcizadas.
El mar, que parecía al principio
vacilar, al fin ha entrado
en las habitaciones y ha dejado
en lo oscuro un prisma luminoso.

¿Habrá – en alguna parte –
un trampolín fantasma
del cual tirarse al mar mas acabar
ahogándose en el cielo?
¿O de otra suerte descender
al fondo del océano
donde un afán no confesado
pueda hallar el olvido?

Tantas cosas se escuchan
que nunca fueron dichas.
¡Qué soledad! ¡Qué premio inacabable
de aislamiento que, sin embargo,
no implica privación!
Se puede ver ese silencio.
Merece una respuesta
y esparce visos y reflejos.

Aquí se encuentra la vacante delatora,
el axiómetro vacío,
la oquedad que induce y calma
con precisión cual un espejo,
la esencia que resume la sustancia,

82

LOOKING FOR THE HORSE LATITUDES

After the painting Rooms by the Sea
by Edward Hopper

Something unseen weighs heavy
on the resilience of the mind.
The usual apparitions
have all been exorcised.
The sea that seemed at first
to hesitate has come
at last into the rooms
leaving in the dark a wedge of light.

Is there – somewhere –
a spectral springboard
from which one might jump
into the sea
and yet drown in the sky?
Or else fall to the ocean floor
where unconfessed anxiety
can find oblivion?

So many things are heard
and yet were never said.
What solitude! What endless prize
of isolation that is not,
surprisingly, bereft!
Such silence can be seen.
It begs response and scatters
glimmers of reflection.

Here lies the telltale vacancy,
the vacant compass.
The emptiness that lures and cries
with mirror-like precision,
the essence that absorbs all substance,

la invertida visión ya corregida
y por encima de la brújula desviada.

¿Podríamos caer en el color
y disolvernos en mera liquidez?
¿Es el espacio el puro y primo
gobernante del mirar,
de modo que no hay ímpetu que lleve
a alguna parte más que allí,
descubrimiento y predestinación?

Aquellas gentes, sí, las multitudes
aquí ausentes, hoy están tan solas.
Anhelan el misterio capaz de presentar
lo que sería el futuro de un pasado.
Están tan solas y por consiguiente
una puerta se ha dejado abierta
silenciosamente,
a fin de que ellas y nosotros todos
clavemos la mirada en el sonido
y algún día, cansados ya del paredón
del tiempo, zarpemos con el viento hacia la calma.

inverted vision turned aright
past the axiometer's deflection.

Could one fall into color
and dissolve in sheer liquidity?
Is space the pure and primal
ruler of our eyes,
so that no surge can lead
to anywhere but there,
to preordained discovery?

Those people, yes, the crowds
who are not here, they are so lonely
they crave the mystery
that can present a future of the past.
They are so lonely, and thus a door
has been left open quietly
that they and we and all can gaze
into the sound and some day,
when weary of the walls of time,
set sail and ride the wind toward the night.

ODA A SAFO

ODE TO SAPPHO

A SAFO: TRES RECUERDOS ONÍRICOS

Fue preciso conversar con las estrellas
en las noches de verano, con la luna,
con las montañas y las piedras,
con las aves y los árboles egeos
para dar con las palabras
que hicieran posible el explicarme
ante tus ojos biselados,
tu amplia frente de cariño ambiguo,
tu perfil callado,
tus labios desdeñosos y ambarinos.

Crecieron mis anhelos y temores.
El mágico recuerdo de un idilio
que inconsciente me buscaba,
sediento y húmedo como las sales
que las olas llevan, me condujo
como un mapa de sanguíneos vasos
afluentes de ansiedad y mariposas,
a inyectar como un Asclepio futurista
de jóvenes audacias, colores desmedidos,
azules y escarlatas en pensamientos ávidos
que fueron dardos disparados a tu pecho.

La veloz Artemisa,
arreando los corceles de la aurora,
pasó por el boscaje deslumbrante
que nubla la visión de los mortales.
Contemplé la sombra fugitiva
que sigue siempre al tránsito divino.
Mas el efecto breve fue
pues mi ilusión era otra: todo estaba
cifrado en el vago misterio, el prodigio
brumoso de una noble osadía.

TO SAPPHO: THREE DREAM-MEMORIES

I needed conversations with the stars
during the summer nights, with the moon,
with the mountains and the rocks,
with the birds and the Aegean trees
in order to find words
that would allow me to express myself
before your chiseled eyes,
your simple forehead of ambiguous love,
your quiet profile,
your disdainful amber lips.

My longing and my apprehension grew.
The magic memory of an interlude
that unconsciously pursued me,
thirsting and dewy like the salt
carried by the waves, led me,
like a map of sanguine vessels
lavish in anxiety and butterflies,
a youthful and daring
Asclepius of the future, to inject
voluptuous colors, scarlet and blue
in avid meditations
which became arrows shot into your bosom.

Swift Artemise,
herding the steeds of dawn,
passed through the dazzling thicket
that clouds the vision of us mortals.
I beheld the flowing shadow
that always follows the divine kinesis.
But my purpose was another: everything
depended on the unaccountable mystery,
the opaque fascination of a noble presumption.
Dreams are confused with expectations.

Los sueños se confunden con las esperanzas.
La memoria juega con las ilusiones.
Mis ansias desafiaron mares y aplanaron montes.
Así fue como los años, siglos y milenios
renacieron días y horas, minutos y segundos.
El trompo de los cielos consumó su éxtasis.
Se conjugaron los cuerpos y las almas
en verbos para siempre irrepetibles
al dar mis pensamientos flechas
en el blanco de tu mármol carne,
en la materia oscura de tus sentimientos.

Primer recuerdo...
Las aguas del pequeño río
corrían bajo las ramas de membrillo.
Las rosas silvestres velaban el valle
con su sombra, y el follaje
engendraba un sueño sin visiones.
La vega en que pastaban los caballos
rebosaba con la floración del trébol
y los capullos de anís desparramaban
una suavísima fragancia.

En un acto de ritual campestre,
las muchachas que eran tus discípulas
bailaban con un ritmo lento
alrededor de un viejo altar.
Sus delicados pies pisaban con asombro
la dulce alfombra hecha de flores.
Y tú invocaste a la ciprina Venus
y le ofrendaste unas guirnaldas.
Escanciamos el jugo de toda una cosecha
y, para amenizar la fiesta,
con tus dedos gráciles lo saturaste
con un néctar en las copas de oro.

Memory plays with make-believe.
My eagerness defied the seas and the razed mountains.
Thus years, centuries, millennia
were reborn days and hours, minutes, seconds.
The spinning-top of heaven reached its ecstasy.
Bodies and souls were conjugated
in verbs forever unrepeatable
when the arrows of my thoughts
hit the target of your marble flesh,
the dark substance of your sentiments.

The first memory…
The waters of the little stream
flowed beneath the branches of the quince tree.
The wild roses covered the valley
with their shades, and the foliage
produced an imageless slumber.
The lowland where the horses grazed
was teeming with the growth of clover
and the anise spread
its velvet fragrance.

In an act of agrestic ritual,
the girls who were your pupils
danced in slow rhythm
around an ancient altar,
their dainty feet stepping shyly
on the elysian carpet made of flowers.
And you invoked the ciprine Venus,
offering her some garlands.
We decanted the juice of a whole harvest
and to make the feasting more agreeable,
with your graceful hands
you flavored it with nectar
in the golden cups.

A tu querida Dica le recomendaste
que trenzara sus cabellos con jacintos,
sabiendo que la Diosa siempre atiende
a quienes lucen adornos apacibles
y así reciben los favores de las Gracias.
La niña que te acompañaba era muy bella:
su cuerpo hecho de flores y de luces.
Yo sospeché que no la habrías cambiado
por toda Lesbos, por toda Lidia,
por todo el oro de su rey. Y sin embargo,
supe después que había habido un momento,
hacía ya cierto tiempo y lejos de Cleís,
en que te consumió un gran amor por Atis,
cuya pasión pertenecía a Andrómeda,
y que también Girina te dejó esperando
en otra soledad como un abismo,
como el Euripo Pireo. Y llegué a saber
que entonces añoraste el alivio de la muerte,
deshecha en llanto, sola y olvidada,
puesto que Girina te había dicho:
"Safo, qué angustia hemos sufrido,
y ahora te voy a abandonar,"
y que tú le habías amonestado:
"Anda, sé feliz y piensa en mí.
Nos quisimos tiernamente. Déjame hacerte
recordar que saboreamos lo más bello
y lo más dulce". Mas ya presentirías que Eros,
el fundidor de muslos, te volvería a ofuscar:
furtivo, agridulce, ineludible.
Ya puesto el sol, la noche ya pasada,
la luna con sus rosados dedos oscurecía
los brillos de innúmeras estrellas
y su propia luz brillaba más que nunca
sobre los prados inundados de capullos
y sobre el mar amargo.
Caía el rocío y las rosas abrían

You urged your dearest Dica
to braid her hair with hyacinths,
knowing that the Godess pays attention
to those who wear wild ornaments
and thus receive the favors from the Graces.
The girl attending you was very beautiful:
her body made of lights and flowers.
I suspected you would not have traded her
for all of Lesbos or the whole of Lydia,
for all the gold that was its king's. And yet
I later learned that there had been a moment,
it was some time before and far then from Cleïs,
when you had been consumed by love for Atthis,
whose passion was Andromeda,
and that Gyrina also abandoned you
in another loneliness like an abyss,
like the Euripian Piraeus. And I came to know
that you longed for the rest that death can bring,
worn out by grief, forgotten and alone,
because Gyrina said to you:
"Sappho, what sorrow have we suffered,
and now I'm going to leave you,"
and you had said to her:
"Go and be happy and think of me.
We loved each other tenderly. Let me remind you
we enjoyed what is most beautiful and sweet".
But you must have already guessed that Eros,
the merger of thighs, would again tempt you:
stealthy, bittersweet, ineluctable.
The sun having set, the night having passed,
the moon with its rosy fingers darkened
the brilliance of innumerable stars
and its own light shone more than ever
on the fields covered with flowers
and on the bitter sea.
Covered with the morning dew the roses

ansiosamente sus corolas.
Reventaba el delicado perifollo
y también el meliloto, mientras que tú
en vaivén deambulabas con tu pena
e invocabas con tus hondos pensamientos
a la hermosa Atis, en tanto que tu corazón,
presa de tu sufrimiento,
se escuchaba claramente en su latido:
"¡Ven a mí, ven a mí"!

Segundo recuerdo...
Bajamos la precipitada cuesta
hasta la cuenca de un arroyo. Allí estaba
un manzanar con altares y ofrendas de incienso.
En la urna estaban las cenizas de Tima,
difunta antes de casarse y transportada
a la sombría casa de Perséfone.
Antes de que la pira se encendiera,
cada una de sus compañeras había cortado
una guedeja de su cabellera
y después la había puesto sobre el túmulo.
En aquel solemne ambiente te escuché decir:
"Cadenas de flores a menudo trenzaste
y las colgaste de tu hermoso cuello;
cientos de aromas allí se mezclaron.
Con un diluvio de fragante mirra,
bálsamo filtrado de los ojos reales,
frecuentemente ungiste el codiciado busto.
Sobre esteras suaves y tupidas,
rodeada de tus servidoras, pronto
habrías logrado suprimir tu deseo de amigas.
No hubo fiesta protalámica
o dedicada a nuestros dioses,
no hubo juego rústico que no hayamos
compartido, Tima. Pero ahora
ningún treno logrará su eco quejumbroso

eagerly opened their corollas.
The chervil was delicately blooming
as was the melilot, while in your pain
you wandered, calling in your deepest thoughts
to the lovely Atthis, and your heart,
imprisoned by affliction,
could be clearly heard while beating:
"Come to me! Come to me!"

The second memory...
We descended the steep bluff
until we reached the river bank. There was
an apple grove with altars and offerings of incense.
In the urn there lay Thyma's ashes,
having died before her wedding and transported
to Persephone's dark house.
Before the pyre was lit
each one of her companions had shorn
a lock of her abundant hair
and had lain it on the funeral pile.
In that solemn setting I heard you say:
"You often braided chains of flowers
and hung them from your lovely neck,
thus blending there hundreds of scents.
With a deluge of sweet-smelling myrrh,
a balsam filtered from the royal eyes,
you often anointed your covetable breasts.
On thick soft quills, amid your servants,
you soon will have suppressed your need for friends.
There was no wedding feast
nor one dedicated to our gods,
there were no rustic games we didn't share,
Thima. But threnody
will have a gloomy echo

en el sitio donde rendimos homenaje
a las Musas. Ya fue, y yacerás muda y rígida,
y nadie se acordará de ti y cómo fuiste.
Ya nadie anhela tu llegada
y jamás serás de nuevo deleitada
por la rosa pieria. Ya sin fama,
arrojada serás al ámbito donde Hades reina,
y vagarás inquieta entre las multitudes
de silentes sombras. Y, sin embargo,
de Sardes una y otra vez nos llegan
tus pensamientos como palomas mensajeras.
Cómo gozamos juntas nuestros días.
Cómo Arignota, embelesada por tu encanto,
te siguió a través de todos los peligros,
sí, como si fueras una diosa".
Tal fue tu rezo fúnebre por tu querida amiga.

Tercer recuerdo...
Sé que en la oscuridad oí vibrar tu voz:
"La luna ha desaparecido, también las Pléyades.
La mitad de la noche ha llegado a su término.
Sobre mi lecho yazgo sola. Eros
ha destrozado mis sentidos
como una tempestad que desde la montaña
desciende a través de la floresta.
Afrodita inmortal, entronizada en esplendor,
hija traviesa del Padre Zeus, te ruego
por lo que tú más quieras no agobiar
mis ansias con angustia y sufrimiento.
Hazme una visita como antaño,
responde a mi llamado desde lejos.
Deja la morada de tu Padre
y alista tu carruaje deslumbrante.
Apresúrate a venir. Pinzones reales

in the site where we now render homage
to the Muses. It's over. You will be mute and rigid
and no one will remember you nor how you were.
Now no one longs for your arrival
and nevermore will you be feted
with the Pierian roses. Now unrecognized,
you will be thrust to the place where Hades reigns,
and you will wander restless among multitudes
of silent shades. And yet,
from Sardis we still perceive your thoughts
like carrier pigeons.
How we enjoyed our days together.

How Arignota, enchanted by your beauty,
followed you through all the dangers,
yes, as if you were a goddess."
Such was your wonderful prayer
for your cherished friend.

Third memory…
I know that in the dark I heard your voice resound:
"The moon has disappeared, so have the Pleiades.
Half the night has reached its limit.
I lie alone upon my bed. Eros
has destroyed my senses
like a storm that from the mountaintop
descends across the wooded fields.
Immortal Aphrodite, enthroned in splendor,
playful daughter of Father Zeus, I beg you
please do not burden my anxiety
with anguish and dejection.
Come visit me as once you did,
answer my supplication from afar.
Leave your Father's court
and make your carriage ready.
Make haste to come. Royal chaffinches

serán tus guías por esta Tierra:
miles de alas sesgadas hacia abajo
desde el etéreo y refulgente cielo.
Rápido será tu vuelo y tú, Señora,
preguntarás, sonrientes tus eternos labios,
qué es lo que hoy nuevamente me aflige,
por qué mi pobre boca te ha invocado,
qué es lo que este loco corazón desea
que le concedas. Por eso tú dirás:
"¿quién te ha ofendido, Safo,
a quién ha enmarañado Peito
en las redes de tu amor?
Quien te rehuye luego te perseguirá,
quien te rechaza luego se te ofrecerá,
quien hoy desdeña tu pasión
mañana se te entregará aunque no quiera.
Y yo te pido, oh Diosa,
que otra vez suavices mi tristeza.
Sé mi aliada como antaño
en esta guerra dentro de mi corazón".
Yo recuerdo claramente esos sucesos.
Podría haber sido no por cierto Cércolas,
casual esposo tuyo y padre de tu hija,
sino aquel hombre a quien tú descubriste
sentado frente al dios de la lujuria,
aquel a quien hubieras querido retener
y no pudiste ni siquiera conocer por miedo
a que no fuera suficiente,
a que no fuera igual al dios
que avivaba tus ojos y tus ingles.
Antes que tú lo confesaras, me di cuenta
que suponías haber prendido mis deseos
y, sin embargo, no podías haber sabido
que hubiesen sido para ti tan solamente.
Antes que tú lo susurraras, yo lo supe,
sin percibir tu infancia en Mitilene,
sin sospechar tu condición privilegiada.

will guide you through the Earth:
a thousand wings all downward bent
from the ethereal and refulgent sky.
Their flight will be so swift and you, my Lady,
your lips with their eternal smile, will ask
why is it this poor voice invokes you,
what is it this mad heart desires you
to grant me. And that is why you'll ask:
'Who has offended Sappho,
who has become enamored by Peitho
in the spring-nets of your love?
Whoever flees you will later give you chase,
whoever shuns you will later volunteer,
whoever spurns your passion
tomorrow will surrender want or not.
And I beseech you, oh Goddess, please
to once again soften my sorrow.
Be my ally as you were before
in this war so deep within my heart'.

I still remember all that clearly.
I could have been, though certainly not Cercolas,
your casual husband and father of your daughter
rather that other man you once discovered
seated before the god of appetites,
the one you would have wanted to retain
and could not even know for fear
of his not being equal to the god
who enlivens your visions and your loins.
Before you could confess it, I knew
that you discovered having lit a fire
in me, and yet you could not know
it would have been for you alone.
Before you might have whispered it, I knew it,
though unaware of your infancy in Mytilene,
and unaware of your privileged condition.

Tu lengua se quebraba en tiernos fuegos
que estremecían tu piel tornasolada,
tus ojos grises, incapaces hoy de verme,
tus oídos casi ahogados en oleajes inauditos,
el sudor que parecía inundar tu cuerpo,
los estremecimientos por la fiebre intermitente,
la palidez de yerba seca que sufriste,
casi locura de no poder amar como querías.
Todas esas cosas yo las supe
porque hoy las siento y las he vivido.
Al fin logré el tremendo atrevimiento,
pero ya es tarde. Tan pronto desapareciste.
Desapareció tu carne. Sus visos desaparecieron.
Mas tu divina voz prosigue melancólica:
"Ay, virginidad, virginidad, has huido
de mí y ya no seré tuya jamás...
Aquellos a quienes he favorecido
me han hecho el mayor daño...
Lo bello es bueno, y quien es bueno
pronto será igualmente bello...
La noche logra que todo vuelva a su redil,
todo lo que la aurora dispersó
con su brillante luz de noche vuelve:
la oveja, la cabra, todas
las criaturas vuelven a sus madres...
Así cual los pastores con sus pesados pies
atropellan los jacintos, los manojos
de púrpura son aplastados en el llano...
Así cual la granada se enrojece
allá muy alto en la copa del granado,
allá en la altura última, olvidada
por los cosecheros: de ningún modo olvidada
porque nunca lograron alcanzarla...
Sólo en vosotras pienso, las hermosas,
inmutables para siempre..."

Your tongue then trembled with a tender ardor,
making the color of your skin to change
your somber eyes which cannot see me now,
your ears half drowned in surging sounds,
the sweat that seemed to flood your body,
the shudders caused by intermittent fever,
near lunacy for not being able to give love
the way you wished. All that I knew
for having felt and having lived it.
I finally achieved the great adventure,
but it's too late. Suddenly you disappeared.
Your flesh vanished. Its semblance disappeared.
And yet the marvel of your voice can still be heard:
"Oh, virginity, virginity, you have fled from me
and I will be no longer yours…
Those whom I have favored
have done me the most harm…
The beautiful is good, and who is good
will soon be beautiful…
Night gets all back into its fold,
everything the dawn dispersed
with its bright light returns at night:
the lamb, the goat, all creatures
to their mothers do return…
Thus like the shepherds with their heavy feet
trample the hyacinths, the bunches
of burdock are flattened in the fields…
Thus like the pomegranate reddens
up high atop of the pomegranate tree,
up there on the highest branch, forgotten
by the harvesters: not at all forgotten
because they could not reach it…
I think of you only, the beautiful ones,
immutable forever…"

Te recuerdo como el sabor de esa granada
que huye por mi paladar aliento arriba,
dejando su cariño soñoliento
que luego desconozco en tus secretos,
porque hoy te encuentro convertida en piedra.
Nuestro idilio duró lo que un relámpago
lanzado entre dos fases de lo inconmensurable.
La vida no concuerda con el tiempo
si mutuamente se trascienden y se excluyen.

No te tiraste al mar como dice la leyenda.
Las leyendas nunca cuentan
lo que realmente sucedió.
Una tormenta se erigió en el mar convulso.
Se rayó el horizonte de cristales y clamores.
Y el espacio indeciso, ágil de relinchos
y lánguido de flores,
siguió su trayectoria hacia el olvido.

I remember like the taste of that pomegranate
that rushes up my palate,
leaving behind its dreamy fondness
which I fail to recognize in your enigma,
because I find you now turned into stone.
Our idyll lasted as a bolt of lightning
hurled between two phases of the measureless.
Life cannot be in accord with time
when they transcend or just avoid each other.

You didn't throw yourself into the sea
as legend goes.
Legends never tell what really happened.
A storm arose on the convulsive ocean.
Crystals and clamors furrowed the horizon.
And the hesitant space, teeming
with agile neighing
and with languid flowers,
followed its course toward oblivion.

GIOVINEZZA

GIOVINEZZA

PALOMA PÁLIDA // MUJER MORENA

Acércate indecisa, suspicaz, prudente //
toca mi mano descuidadamente //
busca aquello que tu instinto exige //
saluda con tu voz de madre niña //
picotea ¿qué es lo que encuentras?
¿migas de pan, semillero de alpiste?
parco sustento para tanto arrullo //
parlotea ¿qué es lo que inventas?
¿música de ángeles, nido de imágenes?
sonidos suaves con que me embelesas //
frisa mis dedos con tu pico, no,
no dejes que acaricie tu cabeza,
tu cola de plumas pizarreñas //
roza mi cara con la tuya, no,
ni eso siquiera, allega apenas
tu frescura al calor de mi deseo //
y salta, coquetea trazando un arco
para volver al foco de tu esquema //
y ríe, contempla de manera esquiva
mi rapto inútil ante tu belleza //
aléjate otra vez, cual si el peligro
de más intimidad amedrentara
tu fiel, tu tan sutil premisa //
guarda distancia, disimula un tanto
a lo que no te atreves y, sin embargo,
quieres sin saber por qué ni cómo //
clava tu pupila roja en el negror
de mis fantasmas //
clava tu pupila azul en el blancor
de mis amagos //
y dejándote llevar por tu destino //
destino tú y por llevar te dejas //
de repente abre las alas
o lentamente abre los brazos.

PALE DOVE // DARK WOMAN

Come, tentative, suspicious, prudent //
touch my hand carelessly //
look for what your instinct needs //
greet me with your voice of mother-child //
peck around, what do you find?
bread crumbs perhaps, a sesame bed?
scanty sustenance for so much cooing //
with your talk, what do you invent?
music of angels, an imaginary nest?
gentle sounds with which you enchant //
curry my fingers with your beak, yet no,
don't let me touch either your head or
your tail of slate-coloured feathers //
bring your face close to mine, yet no,
not even that, barely approach
your freshness to the heat of my desire //
and skip, flirt as you trace an arc
and then return to your very starting point //
and laugh, as you coyly behold
my useless rapture that your beauty makes //
withdraw again, as if the danger
of greater closeness frightened
your firm and subtle ways //
stay distant, dissemble some
what you don't dare and yet
you wish not knowing why nor how //
fix your crimson pupil on the blackness
of my phantoms //
fix your azure pupils on the whiteness
of my promise //
and allowing destiny to guide you //
you being destiny and so your lead //
suddenly spread your wings
or slowly open your arms.

GIOVINEZZA

Me pregunto si tú misma estás consciente
de una llama profunda y escondida.
¿Dónde?
¿Dónde hallar el natural imán
que atrae las almas afortunadas
o el esmeril que afila el acero
de las miradas inevitables?
¿Cómo responderías
al roce de una pluma que fuera mi suspiro
en una habitación apenumbrada
por las cortinas que resguardan
el balcón abierto,
en una finca olvidada por el tiempo,
si en un crepúsculo violado yo violara
el pacto de tu consentimiento?
¿Me quemarías
o serías igual que tu vaivén
ante el vuelo de mi pensamiento?
Todavía hoy responderás como antes
a las caricias minuciosas de tu amante,
actos que me están vedados
como a la luna el mediodía.
Dices amor con la sinceridad y la confianza
de una criatura bella,
que conoce apenas la orilla del misterio,
del agudo escalofrío que no revela la experiencia
sino la fantasía.
Como ánade que nada
sobre la superficie cristalina de la casi nada
que es la realidad diaria y ceñida,
te vas y vuelves puntualmente.
Llegas a esa orilla y la rehuyes,
a ese límite

GIOVINEZZA

I wonder if you are yourself aware
of a deeply hidden flame.
Where?
Where is the magnet to be found
that can attract fortunate souls
or the whetstone-sharpened steel
that makes unavoidable glances?
How would you respond
to the brush of the feather
that could be my sigh
in a room darkened by the shutters
covering an open balcony,
in a country house forgotten by time
if, in a violet twilight I dared to violate
the pact to which you did consent?
Would you set me on fire
or would it be the same as when you waver,
knowing the inclination of my mind?
Now you must respond as always
to your lover's meticulous caresses,
acts to me forbidden as midday to the moon.
You say love with the sincerity and trust
of a beautiful creature
who barely knows the edge of mystery,
of the sharp shudder
revealed not by experience
but by fantasy.
Like a waterfowl gliding
on the crystal surface
of the next to nothing
that is everyday reality,
you leave and return punctually.
You reach the brink and then reject it,
that limit

que es la vejez que en mí te aguarda
cargada de ilusiones desleídas
y que, cuando yo ya no esté,
en un crepúsculo violado
y demasiado tarde, conocerás un día.

of old age that in me waits for you,
laden with faded hopes
and that, with me no longer
in a violet twilight
and too late,
one day you'll know.

EL AUSENTE

¿Cómo serás de noche?
Te conozco de mañana, al mediodía y por la tarde.
Pero nunca te he visto de noche
ni a las altas horas de la madrugada.
No sé si yo podría reconocer entonces
tu mirada, tu sonrisa, tus palabras,
o si a la medianoche eres otra muchacha.

¿Cómo serás de noche?
Me desespero por no saber cómo eres
a la hora en que la luna alterna
maliciosamente sus rayos y sus sombras
y en las copas de los árboles,
arrullado por los ecos de las aves,
se mece el sueño que conoces pero desatiendes,
entregada a sentimientos inimaginables.

Tus ojos ¿lucirán con brillos diferentes?
Tus labios ¿serán más tiernos o serán traviesos?
Tu cuerpo entero, libre de ropas,
¿acaso flotará como sirena suspendida
en un mar cuyas caricias son las olas?

En la oscuridad, ya sea sentada
junto a tu balcón
o acostada en tu lecho
sola o acompañada
¿cómo serás a medianoche?
¿Cómo te sentirá la soledad
o el que amorosamente te acompaña?
Yo sólo sé cómo se siente
quien a esa hora está y estará ausente.

THE ABSENT ONE

What must you be like at night?
I know you in the morning, at noon and afternoon.
But I've never seen you at night
or in the early hours around daybreak.
I don't know if then I'd recognize
your look, your smile, your words
or if at midnight you are another girl.

What must you be like at night?
I despair not knowing what you're like
at the time when the moon maliciously
varies its beams and its shadows
and on the tops of the trees,
lulled by the echoes of birds,
rocks the sleep you know but disregard,
having surrendered to unimaginable thoughts.

Would your eyes shine with another brilliance?
Would your lips be tender or mischievous?
Your whole body without its clothing,
would it be like a mermaid that's suspended
by a sea whose waves are its caresses?

In the darkness, whether seated
by a window
or lying in your bed
alone or with someone next to you
what must you be like at midnight?
How would you feel to solitude
or to someone who is lovingly with you?
I only know how that someone feels
who at such hour is and will be absent.

CONFESIÓN

Más allá de la mitad de mi camino te apareces
como una tentación irrealizable,
manojo de deseos incautos,
secreto que en mi vida medra
con ímpetu que lleva hacia la muerte
en una vaga floración de siemprevivas.
Y eres realidad y fantasía.
El aire que te envuelve puebla
mi ambiente sorprendido con destellos.
Avanzo hacia ti en la distancia
de una flor que relumbra,
de una estrella que embriaga.

En una selva ni diáfana ni oscura,
en la rama de un árbol
te encuentro reposada,
pantera que finge no saber su aplomo,
instinto fidelísimo de fiera soberana.
¿Qué quiero contigo? ¿Cómo es que me mandas?
Serán tu integridad mediterránea,
tu juventud con sana vehemencia,
la diligencia que mirando esparces,
el dulce que tu espíritu desgrana.

Pero no es eso todo. Y no es envidia mía.
Quizá no tanto amor como es angustia.

Acaso frágilmente se vislumbre
la razón certera que me atrae.
Un viejo impulso con la oposición
de sexos se combina
y emana del temblor elemental
que dio lugar al mundo,
vuelo viviente que en progenie se define:

CONFESSION

Beyond the middle of my path you now appear
like an impossible temptation,
a handful of gullible desires,
the secret in which my life can prosper
with an impulse that leads toward destruction
in an uncertain blooming of pink flowers.
And you are both reality and fancy.
The air surrounding you peoples
with sparkles my unsuspecting atmosphere.
I go toward you in the distance
of a flower that glitters,
of a star that enraptures.

In a jungle neither dark nor transparent,
on the branch of a tree
I find you resting,
a panther feigning to not know its prudence,
the deepest instinct of a sovereign wildness.
What can I want with you? How is it your command?
Must be Mediterranean virtue,
youth with healthy vehemence,
the diligence you spread when gazing,
the sweetness that your spirit scatters.

But that's not all. And it is not my envy.
Perhaps not so much love as it is anguish.

Maybe one can hazily discover
the certain reason that is my attraction.
An ancient urge becomes combined
with sexual opposition
and issues from the elemental tremor
that gave place to the world,
the living flight defined in progeny:

los hijos que tú tienes
y aquellos que yo tuve y nunca tuve,
esfuerzos que se alargan o detienen
como en fatídica genealogía.

Es ése el sentimiento primigenio
que has suscitado en el fondo de mi hombría.
Mi sino se convierte en el espejo
que mi fascinación por ti reclama.
A medianoche, más allá de media vida
y acaso más acá de media muerte,
en lo preñado y horro de mi cuerpo,
en el horror y en el placer de mi alma,
en lo sombrío y lúcido de mi conciencia
la predestinación chozpa sus burlas,
mis merecidas y más graves ironías.

Y aún con esa desazón despierto,
quiero orientarme en este laberinto,
mis ojos como harapos de silencio,
para alcanzar adonde una voz me llama.

Me llama, me incita y me traiciona,
sin saberlo quien habla,
sin saber que me arrastran
sus felinos y mágicos murmullos.
Y en estos pasos que doy hacia la nada
a tientas lucho en un espacio quebrantado,
pues voy en busca de un lecho ya imposible
que en un sinfín de noches he soñado.

the children that you have
and those I had and never had,
efforts that extend and halt
as in oracular genealogy.

Such is the primigenial sentiment
you have aroused at the bottom of my manhood.
My fate becomes the mirror
that my fascination for you claims.
At midnight, beyond midlife
and perhaps this side of middeath,
in what is pregnant and barren of my body,
in the horror and the pleasure of my soul,
in what is somber and lucid of my conscience
predestination gambols with some mockery,
my well deserved and gravest ironies.

And yet with such vexation I awake,
I want to find my bearings in this labyrinth,
my eyes like scraps of silence,
to reach the place from which a voice is calling.

It calls me, incites me and betrays me,
without knowing it who calls,
without knowing that its feline
and magic murmurings will draw me.
And in these steps that lead to nowhere
I grope and struggle in a fractured space
for I'm searching for a bower that I can't invade
and yet of which I've dreamed in endless nights.

LOS SUEÑOS

1

Debes cuidarte mucho de los sueños.
Se piensa que reflejan
nuestros íntimos secretos,
pero no es cierto.
Los sueños nunca son lo que creemos.
No son lo que queremos o pensamos
sino una cosa aparte,
enteramente separada
del conocimiento acostumbrado.
Los sueños muestran cuadros
que no podemos ver despiertos,
en que los padres, los amigos,
los amantes y los desconocidos
se mezclan y confunden
con la necesidad insospechada
de nuestro celo,
fuerza volcada de repente
hacia el abismo de la inconsciencia.

Soñaste que me amabas.
Lo has confesado.
Que me amabas como a un padre
listo a deparar consejos y cariños.
Sentada en mi regazo estabas
en una habitación oscurecida
de una casa de campo.
¿Te acuerdas?
Sentías extrañas emociones,
gozabas sensaciones sorprendentes
que hoy aún no puedes comprender.
Y auscultabas tu propio corazón,
cuyos latidos quizá eran símbolos

DREAMS

1

You must be very careful of your dreams.
It is thought that they reflect
our most intimate secrets,
but it's not true.
Dreams are never what we think.
They are neither what we wish nor what we think,
they are something else.
Something quite apart
from our accustomed knowledge.
Dreams show pictures
which we can't see when we're awake,
in which parents, friends,
lovers and strangers
mingle and become confused
in the unsuspected need
of our suspicions,
a force thrown suddenly
to the abyss of our unconscious.

You once dreamed that you loved me.
You have confessed it.
That you loved me like a father
ready to give you counsel and caresses.
You were sitting on my lap
in a darkened room
of a country house.
Do you remember?
You felt curious emotions,
you enjoyed surprising feelings
which even now you cannot comprehend.
And you listened to your heart,
where beats perhaps were symbols

de indecisión o de extravío.
Mas todo lo borró la luz del día.
Todo y todos volvieron a su sitio.
Desvanecieron las visiones
pero quedaron pesadumbres imprevistas.
¿Qué hiciste entonces?

2

Hay que tener cuidado con los sueños.
Son los momentos que vivimos
más intensamente aunque siempre
al roce de la sombra
de la memoria.
En su función nada es casual,
no hay accidentes.
Parecen vagos pero son precisos,
preciosos
y libres pero no inocentes.
Son medallones afectivos
que al cabo pierden su relieve,
porque el tiempo
que desgasta piedras y metales
acaba por borrar el cuño delicado
de los sueños.
Lástima que no se pueda hacer
una alcancía con ellos.

Soñé que tú me amabas.
No cual la hija que quisieras ser
o la esposa que quisiera yo,
sino como una amante
que a mi lado recostada,
junto a un balcón abierto aunque cegado por tapices,

of indecision and misconduct.
Yet everything became erased by daylight.
One and all returned to its right place.
Visions disappeared
but there remained an unexpected sorrow.
What did you do then?

2

We must be very careful of our dreams.
They are the moments which we live
with most intensity though always
barely touching the shadow
of a memory.
In their function nothing is by chance,
there are no accidents.
They may seem vague but they are quite precise,
precious,
and free but never innocent.
They are affectionate medallions
sooner or later losing their relief,
because time
that wears down stones and metals
ends up razing the delicate coin
of dreams.
Pity we can't save them
in a coin bank.

I dreamed that you did love me.
Not like the daughter you would want to be
or the wife I wanted you to be,
but like a lover
lying by my side,
next to an open balcony
though blinded by brocades,

alternativamente
me anegaba en las aguas de sus ojos
y me quemaba desnudando las sonrisas
en un ritual interminable.
Y yo sentía extrañas emociones,
gozaba sensaciones sorprendentes
no conocidas antes.
Mi oscuro despertar se acompañó
de una sutil zozobra,
deliquio y a la vez deseo
de seguir soñando.

3

Silencio, por favor.
                    No despertar.
                                        No usar palabras.
Los sueños simplemente son.

alternatively
drowning me in the water of your eyes
and burning me while denuding smiles
in a ritual without end.
And I felt strange emotions,
enjoying such sensations
I had never known before.
A dark awakening came to me
along with a subtle anguish,
an ecstasy and a desire
to go on dreaming.

3

Silence, please.
        Do not wake up.
                Do not use words.
Dreams simply are.

RESPUESTA

¿Qué esperar, entonces,
si acaso por fin nos percatamos
de que lo que una vez quisimos
sigue siendo lo que hoy queremos
como nostalgia de un edén perdido?

¿Qué esperaremos en estas circunstancias
de un nuevo encuentro con una rosa abierta,
no ya un capullo sino una flor
en su más amplia posibilidad de encanto,
vigor y ofrecimiento,
vorágine de luz y de perfume,
alta marea de un implacable anhelo
que desconcierta los sentidos
y aun la expectativa más recóndita?
Semejante esperanza nos confunde
el paradigma de los sentimientos,
turba la paz y produce quimeras.

Pues la felicidad siempre será la misma,
un duende bueno, querencioso,
que se hospeda en temporales exquisitos.
Es una realidad,
pero una realidad huidiza, frágil, inestable
como el soplo de los vientos
que peregrinamente vienen desde lejos,
y su estación es cuando más la de un ensalmo,
apenas apto para obligar horas tranquilas.

¿Hay que quedar conformes
con la brevedad de estas visitas?
¿A quién dirijo esta querella endeble,
esta consolación que no merece
una respuesta
al igual retórica por vana?

REPLY

What, then, can we expect
if we have come to realize
that what we once desired
continues being so today
like the longing of a lost paradise?

What can we expect in these circumstances
of a new encounter with a blossomed rose
no longer a mere bud but a full flower
in its most ample possibility of charm,
of strength and of surrender,
a vortex of light and fragrance,
high tide of a relentless longing
that obscures the senses
and surely the most secret hope?
Such expectation can confuse
our model sentiments,
it can disturb the peace and nurture folly.

For happiness will always be the same,
it is a gentle little elf
living in delightful seasons.
It really does exist,
but it is fleeting, fragile, fickle,
like a gust of wind
curiously coming from afar
and its leisure will at most be but a spell,
barely good for wishing peaceful times.

Must we be satisfied
with the transience of these visits?
To whom do I address this feeble plaint,
this lamentation that does not deserve
reply
being so grandiloquent and vain?

Te la dirijo a ti,
desesperante niña de mis ojos ya menguantes,
primavera que a destiempo llega y deposita
en mi letargo
inusitadas sensaciones,
nonio que mide inadvertidamente
mi premura.
A ti te hablo, te canto, te susurro
estas palabras huecas pero inevitables.
Que si las oyes
comprenderás y sentirás tristeza,
sabiendo como solamente tú podrás saberlo,
que no podrás y que no puedes responder
por la felicidad que no es la tuya.

I'm addressing it to you,
maddening apple of my eye despite my age,
springtime coming late and leaving
the most unusual feelings
in my lethargy,
unnoticed instrument that measures my ambition.
It is you I speak to, sing to you, and whisper
these hollow yet inevitable words.
For if you hear them
you'll understand and feel my sadness,
knowing as only you will know
that you can never be responsible
for a happiness that is not yours.

FIN DE JORNADA

Non c' è futuro,
c' è solo passato.

— Cinema Paradiso

Hemos llegado al fin de la jornada.
Hemos llegado hasta este punto
en que coinciden
nuestro espacio y nuestro tiempo
como los arcos de un atardecer
en que muy poco a poco
ha ido declinando
la relación visual de dos esferas,
no obstante que el calor se siente
más íntensamente
como queriendo desafiar
la inevitable oscuridad del cielo.

Hasta este punto
nuestros pies nos han traído
por no se sabe qué sentido
de existencia.
¿Cómo pudo ser que comulgáramos
desde el principio,
cuando nos vimos a través de las edades,
sabiendo que no había razón
y que no habría más que un suspenso
en la querencia?

Aire, tierra, agua y fuego,
piedras, plantas y animales,
todo eso conjugándose en la especie
se ha abstraído en un segundo génesis
que frena aún para nosotros
su transcurso momentáneamente.
En este instante en que no hay estrellas

JOURNEY'S END

> *Non c'è futuro,*
> *c'è solo passato.*
> — Cinema Paradiso

We have reached our journey's end.
We have reached the very point
where our time and our space
can coincide
like the arcs of evening
in which the visual correlation of two spheres
has been slowly declining,
although the warmth is felt
much more intensely
as if wanting to defy
the inevitable darkness of the sky.

Up to this point
our feet had brought us
through we know not what bearing
of existence.
How could it be that we communed
from the beginning,
having seen each other through our ages,
knowing that there was no reason
and that there would be nothing but suspense
in our affection?

Air, earth, water and fire,
rocks, plants and beasts
a conjugation of the species
which has become abstracted in a second genesis
and for an instant and our benefit
bridles it's evolution.
At this moment when there are no stars

que incitaran una impropia alternativa,
y para no caer de nuevo en el abismo,
para salvar el corazón de este universo
que nosotros solos conocemos,
palpitante y único,
debemos detenernos,
mirando atrás y no adelante,
y mirándonos reconocer
que ya hemos sido,
que somos pero no seremos,
que hemos llegado triunfal y noblemente
hasta este punto,
al fin de la jornada.
Y ahora,
uno del otro desapareceremos.

that might incite improper choices,
and so as not to fall again in the abyss,
to save the center of this universe
which alone we know,
alive yet unrevealed,
we now must stop.
And looking back instead of forward,
look at each other
and admit
that we now have been,
that we are but will not be,
that nobly and triumphantly
we've reached this point,
our journey's end.
And so
one from the other
we shall disappear.

CODA

Y cuando te hayas ido,
cuando hayas desaparecido
como un espejismo,
como un ave de paso,
pájaro fugaz que sin querer has sido
para mí,
o como un celaje solferino
que puso su color efímero
en mi veranillo de San Martín,
habrás dejado y dejarás en tu lugar
la esencia del vacío,
la ausencia de sorpresas y sonrisas,
la desaparición de signos indescifrables.

Se habrá esfumado todo lo querido,
y lo imaginado
será sólo un recuerdo solitario
de lo que no pudo haber sido,
remanso de pasión y de suspenso,
un aire de evasión
que impele el viento
del invierno
y que se desenvuelve como un remolino
en la morbosidad de los suspiros
al borde de una lánguida laguna,
en medio de llanuras tan lejanas
que llegan hasta el fin del mundo
y que visita
muy de cuando en cuando
tan sólo un ciervo gemebundo.

CODA

And when you have gone,
when you have disappeared
like a mirage,
like a bird of passage,
a fleeting bird that unknowingly
you have been for me,
or a scudding cloud bluish-red in hue
that left its evanescent color
in my Indian Summer,
you will have left instead of you
the essence of the void,
the absence of surprises and of smiles,
the disappearance of signs and of enigmas
which then forever will remain a riddle.
Everything loved thus will have vanished
and everything imagined
will have become a lonely memory
of that which could not be,
an eddy of passion and suspense,
a climate of evasion
blown by the winter
wind
spinning like a whirlwind
in the tender mercies of my sadness,
on the edge of a listless lake
in the middle of a plain so far away
that it reaches the world's end
and is visited
only now and then
by a bewailing stag.

CLAVES PARA UNA ANUNCIACIÓN
— a Tita

KEYS TO AN ANNUNCIATION
— to Tita

LA CABEZA A PÁJAROS

Los poetas a menudo han aludido
a esas criaturas por ellos envidiadas:
las aladas.
Y se comprende. Todos quisiéramos volar
porque la gravedad ofende.
Mas no es lo mismo volar en aeroplano
que ser pájaro.
Las alas del avión conquistan el espacio
en tanto que las alas de las aves
lo enamoran.
Lo pajarero me entusiasma tanto
que la jaula de mi cráneo me da espanto,
pues requiero una visión tan plena
como la de una ventana abierta.
Del águila yo me imagino
las poderosas alas capaces de atreverse
con la luz del sol y las sombras de la luna.
Del gavilán admiro el clavado mortífero
como ballesta que se descarga entera.
Cuál será mi fortuna
que en el búho percibo un guiño
que tiene mucho de viejo y algo de niño,
y en la alondra claramente escucho
músicas que se acercan y se alejan
como deliquios.

Del cuervo sospecho que su negación sajona
esconde una carroña.
El colibrí, pájaro mosca, tominejo, picaflor,
chupamirto o chuparrosa me parece
un melómano y extático derviche
que en el crepúsculo embebece.
Del zenzontle y del quetzal ni hablar:
éste es todo color y aquél es todo cantar.

A HEAD FULL OF BIRDS

Poets have often alluded to
those creatures they envy so:
the winged ones.
And it makes perfect sense. We all would fly,
for gravity offends.
Yet it isn't the same to go by plane
as it is to be a bird.
The aircraft's wings conquer the skies
while the wings of birds
make love to the air.
The bird-catcher appeals as much
as my skull-cage terrifies,
since I require a view as complete
as an open window supplies.
I imagine to myself the eagle
with its powerful wings can even brave
the light of the sun, the shade of the moon.
I admire the sparrow-hawk's fatal strike
fired to nail crossbow like.
What will be my fortune
when I perceive the wink of the owl
has much of old age and something of a child,
and in the lark I can clearly hear
a music comes close and recedes
as do ecstasies.

Of the crow I suspect his nay of a Saxon
hides a rotting carrion.
The hummingbird, who's known by many a name –
flower-picker, colibri, rose or myrtle sucker
seems to me an extatic dervish, a sweets-thief,
amuses himself at dawn or dusk.
Of the zenzontle and quetzal, let's not even speak:
the one's all color, the other entirely song.

Las aves son en su conjunto
un gran concierto barroco.
Y porque el canto está hecho de notas
y el vuelo es hermano del baile,
todo en ellos por el aire evoluciona
como en nosotros el alma
que es voz y que es ala, grito y danza.
Y hay otra semejanza
entre las aves y los hombres:
a las unas y a los otros les espera
el juicio al que llaman el final.
Dios condena a los malos pájaros
a rondar cabezas vanas
y premia a los buenos dejándolos desempolvar
las techumbres de su casa.
Esto lo asegura quien lo sabe
(y hace mucho tiempo que lo supe).
Tengo la cabeza a pájaros
porque te llamas Guadalupe
y Aurelia y María. ¡Ave!

Birds in a flock all rehearse
for some baroque grand concert.
And because singing is made of notes
and flight is sister to ballet
everything with them is performed in space
as in us the soul
is voice and wing, cry and dance.
And there is another resemblance
between birds and men:
for those and for these there awaits
what is called the final judgement.
God condemns the evil avi-fauna
to hover above heads full of vain thoughts
and rewards the good by letting them dust
His house's vaulted roofs.
He who knows assures it is so
(and for a long time he's known).
My head is filled with birds because
your name is Guadalupe
and Aurelia and María. Ave!

Translated by Dave Oliphant

SEIS CLAVES PARA UNA ANUNCIACIÓN

1
Anunciación

Pulso una onda inaudita, infinita
pero inmediata
como la cuerda de un instrumento
inconcebible e íntimo,
como reiteración fuera del tiempo,
fraccionada en medidas armoniosas
que sustraen del placer la espera ávida.

La formación fundamental de círculos
concéntricos,
el salmo tan gradual del agua,
gota que de una fuente
cae tras de sí misma,
se prismatiza en luz, color, diafanidad,
espectro resumido en sensaciones
menos recordadas y más adivinadas
como en el sueño
acariciado a la distancia.

El sol despierta. La luna duerme.
Y me confirmo en la existencia
de mis propios sentimientos.
En el cáliz de tu mirada hoy lejana
presiento la forma intacta de la felicidad.

2
Primera

Su sonido se eleva
y al despertar despierta

SIX KEYS TO AN ANNUNCIATION

1
Annunciation

I come upon an unexpected pitch, infinite
and yet immediate
like the string of an instrument
intimate and inconceivable,
like a repetition out of time,
divided in harmonious measures
subtracting from delight the avid waiting.

The fundamental shaping
of concentric circles,
the water's oh so gradual psalm,
each drop from a fountain
that falls after itself
becomes a prism of light, of color, of transparency,
a spectrum summarized as it is divined,
a dream caressed from far away.

The sun awakes. The moon then goes to sleep.
I find assurance in my sentiments.
In the chalice of your gaze now distant
I sense the form unthouched of happiness.

2
One

Its sound rises
and on waking there wakes

en mi conciencia
la inefable sensación que produjera
una campana casi imperceptible
desde un distante campanario,
sensación que apenas se insinúa
mediante el hilo del espacio
que se encoge según se intensifica
el sol de la mañana,
hasta tocarlo todo plenamente
y ser fenómeno predominante
en nuestra estancia.

¿Es tu voz tenue, delgadita acaso?
De ningún modo.
Tu voz es un prodigio por sonora.
Mas su intención se cifra en acuidad
finísima, como una torre esbelta
de rectitud catedralicia
que despunta en espiral de incienso.
Tu voz, amanecer de la luz melódica,
de melodía lumínica,
que poco a poco va filtrándose
por las pupilas del oído:
oído, sonido, luz nunca sombra,
nunca silencio.

3
Segunda

Corona de ovillos casi vellones
de una reina aún no entronizada.
Laberinto libre ya del minotauro,
dispuesto, sin embargo y sin remedio,
a encarcelar en su sosiego
al transeúnte incauto.

within my conciousness
the inexplicable sound coming from
a bell faintly heard
in a distant belltower,
a sound barely perceived
in the thread of space
which shrinks as the moving sun
grows brighter
and touches everything completely,
becoming the prevailing fact in our dwelling.

Could it be your voice, perhaps, delicate and light?
By no means.
Your voice is a model of sonority.
Yet its intent depends on its fine tuning,
like a slender tower, cathedral-like
in its aplomb,
crowned with an incense spire.
Your voice, dawn of melodious light,
of luminous melody,
that slowly filters
through the pupils of the ear:
ear, sound, light never shadow,
never silence.

3
Two

Crown of curls almost locks of wool
of a queen not yet enthroned.
A labyrinth now free of minotaurs
and yet hopelessly disposed
to snare any unwary passerby
in its tranquility.

Mas la hiladilla yace allí para salvar
al Teseo tardío,
al supuesto héroe moribundo
que nunca dejará a su Ariadna.

Mirar tu cabello es perderse
en el oro y la plata de la luna soleada,
perderse y después rescatarse
en una periferia de alborada.
Mirarlo es soñar con solazarse
sobre la mansedumbre
de la piel de un tigre vivo,
ilusión de volutas y de hilos
en la que arde mi ansiedad
con el fuego tranquilo de un amor definido,
que tan pronto muere como se renueva
y que cambia el cautiverio legendario
por un vuelo infinito.

4

Tercera

Hacen del tacto la esencia de la dicha.
Sus dedos van creando
una escalera incandescente,
una vereda múltiple
como una red de estrellas.
Pasan del quehacer insulso
al ejercicio lírico
y al placer repleto de sabores
con naturalidad que asombra.
Van recorriendo el mapa de la vida diaria
y pasan al de la extraordinaria
con la sabiduría y la gracia
de quien se sabe santa.

But the yarn lies there to save
the latter-day Theseus,
the supposedly death-stricken hero
who will never leave Ariadne.

To look at your hair and get lost
in the silver and gold of the sunlit moon,
get lost and then save oneself
in the contours of the dawn.
To look at it is to dream of resting
on the tameness of the skin of a tigress,
undulant illusion of shaggy fur
where my eagerness burns
with the quiet fire of a definite love,
which as quickly dies as it revives,
changing the legendary prison
into an infinite flight.

4
Three

They make of touch the essence of delight.
An incandescent stairway
is created by their fingers,
a plural path
such as a web of stars.
With amazing ease
they go from prosing chore
to lyric exercise
and artful pleasure.
They move across the map of daily life
and enter the extraordinary
with the wisdom and the grace
of one who knows of sainthood.

¡Y la increíble nota que producen
en las cuerdas del silencio,
que claramente no es silencio
sino armonía más honda!
Cuántas edades de ternura
llevan ya reunidas en sus yemas.
Cuántos desastres han frustrado
con su delicada fuerza.
Irán tus manos como golondrinas
por el aire perfumado y claro,
sobre los campos digitales de mi calma,
y anochecidas cerrarán mis ojos,
esclareciendo el dédalo del sueño
y suscitando táctiles plegarias.

5
Cuarta

Incitación al delirio,
resguardan el eros de tus dientes.
Dominan una variedad de idiomas
que no siempre son audibles.
Articulan palabras,
musitan canciones,
despliegan sonrisas
que convidan desvaríos,
ofrecen caricias
que estremecen los sentidos,
y bendicen sorpresas
que se convierten en lirios.
Inimitable su lenguaje ilimitado,
es arte, amor, sabiduría
que se enlazan en un nudo de alegría
y se sueltan levemente
para decir lo que ya ha dicho tu alma,

And the awesome note they strike
upon the strings of silence
which is by no means silence
but a deeper harmony!
So many ages of affection
gathered at their tips.
So many tragedies averted by their graceful strength!
Your hands will fly like swallows
through the clear and fragrant air,
over the digital fields that are my calm.
And come the night will close my eyes,
lighting the daedalus of sleep
and eliciting tactile supplications.

5
Four

Incitement to frenzy
kept in the Eros of your lips
that speak a variety of languages
not always audible.
They form words,
whisper songs,
exhibit smiles
that elicit fascination,
offering caresses
that make the senses shudder
and beatify surprises
blossoming like lilies.
Language unlimited, inimitable,
it is art and love and wisdom
together in a knot of happiness,
loosened lightly to express
what your soul has earlier said,

código y conducto, travesía
hacia un edén
en que una eva y un adán se afincan,
hacia una gloria
en que lo eterno ha vuelto a ser
lo que debía:
materia de las noches y los días.

6
Quinta

Es de noche.
Digo que tu cuerpo está hecho de noche
como la luna.
Apenas se le ve durante el día,
pero en la noche luce
con claridad que es nueva
a la vez que antigua.

Como la luna,
no quiere ya fijarse en cosas transitorias.
Busca la sustancia
de la tierra bañada por el sol
y la ronda suavemente,
la envuelve, con su magia cariciosa,
en un ambiente luminoso que seduce,
al bordar de ensueño
el limo fragmentario de la vida.

Me has brindado tu cuerpo bellamente.
Con parsimonia has logrado aquella entrega,
acto nacido de amplias ilusiones
y lentos albedríos.

the code and means, the passage
to a paradise
where an Adam and an Eve reside,
to a Heaven
where Eternity has once again become
what it should be:
a matter of nights and days.

6
Five

And it is night.
I say your body is made of night
as is the moon.
One barely sees it in the day,
but in the night it shines
with a clarity that's new
and at the same time old.

Like the moon,
it doesn't want to see the transitory.
It seeks the substance
of the earth bathed by the sun
and goes around it softly,
envelops it with its caressing magic
in a luminous atmosphere which can seduce
the fragmentary soil of life
woven in sleep.

You have given me your body gracefully.
You have succeeded the surrender soberly,
such act born of trust and willingness.

También como la luna
tu cuerpo mide las distancias,
con altivez interna, resueltas ya tus dudas,
y en un claro de la oscuridad celeste
se proyectan sus deliquios de hermosura.

7

Sexta

Surgen del sueño
con el verde de una selva sorprendida.
Atisban, divisan, contemplan,
y se vuelven a un pleamar
de amores recordados.
Se abren nuevamente cándidos
como la sal y la dulzura
de madrugadas azules.
Lloran a veces
y sus lágrimas
no son ni vegetales ni marinas.
Están hechas de lluvia.

Creí haberlos hecho míos.
Creí beber sus aguas,
lúcidas y esquivas.
Mas no es así.
Eluden mi afán,
mi estrategia, mi dominio.
Vuelan hacia un pasado oscuro
o hacia un porvenir apenas ponderado.
Tus ojos no viven para mí.
Escapan a mi entendimiento.
Son ajenos a mi mundo.
Tu voz, tus manos, tus labios, tu cabello
y tu cuerpo

Again just like the moon
your body measures distances,
with inner haughtiness, all doubts resolved,
and in a clearing of celestial darkness
I can behold the rapture of your beauty.

7
Six

They rise from sleep
with the green of a jungle taken by surprise.
They look, they discover, they behold,
and then go back to a springtide
of remembered loves.
Again they open candidly
like the salt and the sweetness
of blue daybreaks.
Sometimes they weep
and their tears come from neither earth nor sea.
They are made of rain.

I thought I'd made them mine.
I thought I'd drunk
their shy yet lucid waters.
But it's not so.
They flee my eagerness,
my strategy, my dominance.
They fly toward an obscure past
or toward a future not yet pondered.
Your eyes don't live for me.
They elude my understanding.
They are foreign to my world.
Your voice, your hands, your lips, your hair,
and your body

ya son míos.
Me los has consagrado
y se quedan conmigo.
Me pertenecen como yo te pertenezco.
Pero tus ojos no.
Tus ojos viajan al pasado o al futuro.
Esconden paisajes que no revelarías.
Brillan con un brillo de alas líquidas.
Tus ojos no están nunca quietos.
No están nunca tranquilos.
En su raro extravío
iluminan las sombras.
Su mirada dibuja el dolor del recuerdo.
Vislumbran lo invisible,
estelas de almas tránsfugas,
naufragios de velas fantasmas.
Parecen esperar lo inexistente.
Tus ojos eluden el presente.
Son del color del tiempo.
Tus ojos no pueden atenderme.
Contemplan el viento.

are all mine.
You have dedicated them to me
and so they will remain.
They belong to me as I belong to you.
But not your eyes.
Your eyes travel to the past and to the future.
They hide landscapes you do not reveal.
They shine with a brilliance of liquid wings.
Your eyes are never still.
They are never calm.
In their curious wandering
they kindle the shadows.
Their gaze can depict the pain of remembrance.
They can see the invisible,
the wakes of fugitive spirits,
the wrecks of phantom sails.
They seem to expect the nonexistent.
Your eyes elude the present.
Their color is that of time.
Your eyes cannot attend to me.
They behold the wind.

POEMA DE AMOR

Me gustas cuando hablas.
Me gustas cuando dices
todo aquello que no sé
y todo lo que no sabía.
Me gustas cuando explicas
la verdad de las cosas,
cuando en el aire tiemblan
un albor y una gracia,
cuando te desenvuelves
con tu dulzura de sonido inmerso
en una mezcla de sabor e inteligencia,
cuando te vuelves exégeta y sibila.
Me encantas si en tu voz decantas
tu saber enternecido,
la observación casual que para mí
se torna puro canto
que ya despunta en llamamiento.
Me encantas y me inquietas
si tu discurso se pronuncia
cual visión acústica
y búsqueda sombría,
cuando cuestionas el presente y su destiempo
con cautelosa lucidez tan honda
como un conjuro que a la vez es rezo
que en el silencio encuentra su pregunta.
Me gusta tu armonioso desencanto
del que tan pronto surgen las palabras
que son materia musical de la confianza.
Me gusta tu presentimiento de la historia.
Me gustas por tu amor sonoro, risa y llanto.
Pero también me gustas cuando callas.

LOVE POEM

I like you when you're speaking.
I like you when you say
all those things I do not know
and everything I never knew.
I like you when you tell
the very truth of things,
when in the air there tremble
a beginning and a gracefulness,
when you elaborate a thought
with the sweetness of a sound
immersed in flavor and intelligence,
when you turn prophetess and scholar.
You enchant me when your voice decants
with your tender knowledge
any casual observation
which for me becomes a song
reaching an inspiration.
You enchant me and disquiet me
if your discourse takes the shape
of an acoustic vision
and a somber quest,
when you question the present and its untimeliness
with cautious and profound lucidity
which is at once a prayer and a conjuring
that in the silence finds its element.
I like your congenial disillusions
from which quite soon the words arise
that musically regain your confidence.
I like your intuition regarding history.
I like your verbal love, your laughter and your weeping.
But I also like you when you're quiet.

UN ABRIL PARA TITA

April is the cruelest month...
— *T.S. Eliot*

Quizá no sea posible discernir
lo que atrae el canto de una alondra
a las múltiples estrías de un ágata.
Mas nadie negará el silvestre encanto
que tiene la humilde madreselva,
que muy adentro de la flor se guarda
en el botón mostrenco e ignorado
que une los colores y los ecos
en el atrio de un templo abandonado.

La lluvia dejará su huella evanescente,
cuento oriental de trazo indescifrable,
sobre el canto desdeñado por las aves.
El ocaso extenderá su melodía sanguínea
contra el muro marginal del cielo.
Y la luz que se afina tras la noche
que se amerita en sus cabales y trasuntos
desfía al sentido hasta lograr el último peldaño
de una escala que asciende más allá del mundo.

AN APRIL FOR TITA

April is the cruelest month...
— *T.S. Eliot*

Perhaps it is impossible to tell
what is it that attracts the singing of a lark
to the many striae of an agate.
But no one will deny the simple charm
the honeysuckle has
deep in the flower's consequence,
wild and so ignored
fusing the colors and the echoes
in the atrium of an abandoned temple.

The rain will leave its evanescent tracks,
oriental tale in indecipherable signs,
on stones scorned by the birds.
The sunset will extend its sanguine melody
against the marginal enclosure of the sky.
But the light that is sharpened in the night,
that persists in its replicas and skills,
defies all sense until it claims the final rung
of the ladder that ascends beyond the world.

UN DICIEMBRE PARA TITA

Se ha parado la rueda de la noche...
— *Juan Ramón Jiménez*

...donde el amor inventa su infinito.
— *Pedro Salinas*

Se diría que fuérase a extinguir
la luz del año,
de este breve universo que circunda
el existir de nuestra íntima conciencia,
gajo de sutil insuficiencia
cual de fruta de un edén ya casi efímero.

Mas de pronto han surgido nuevos rayos
que aún auguran ascensiones matutinas
en este mes concreto y promisorio,
mes de veneración e imantamiento,
resurrección allá en el horizonte limpio.
Y se ha parado al fin la rueda de la noche
en ese sitio preciso
donde los ojos de los más devotos
combinan sus colores y sus sueños,
tierra de espíritu de la que dos son dueños,
donde el amor inventa su infinito.

A DECEMBER FOR TITA

Se ha parado la rueda de la noche...
— Juan Ramón Jiménez

...donde el amor inventa su infinito.
— Pedro Salinas

It might be said
that the year's light is about to be extinguished,
the light of this brief universe
surrounding our consciousness's existence,
part of a subtle insufficiency
like the fruit of an Eden near ephemeral.

Yet suddenly new lightning has risen
auguring matinal ascensions
in this concrete and promissory season,
this month of veneration and enchantment,
lightning from a sun refusing conquest,
a resurrection beyond the clear horizon.
And the wheel of night has come full circle
in the specific place
where the most devoted eyes
combine their colors and their dreams,
spiritual earth belonging to the two of us
where love invents the infinite.